BFI Film Classics

MW00467085

The BFI Film Classics is a ~~series of books~~ that introduces, interprets and celebrates landmarks of world cinema. Each volume offers an argument for the film's 'classic' status, together with discussion of its production and reception history, its place within a genre or national cinema, an account of its technical and aesthetic importance, and in many cases, the author's personal response to the film.

For a full list of titles available in the series, please visit our website: <www.palgrave.com/bfi>

'Magnificently concentrated examples of flowing freeform critical poetry.'
Uncut

'A formidable body of work collectively generating some fascinating insights into the evolution of cinema.'
Times Higher Education Supplement

'The series is a landmark in film criticism.'
Quarterly Review of Film and Video

'Possibly the most bountiful book series in the history of film criticism.'
Jonathan Rosenbaum, *Film Comment*

Editorial Advisory Board

Geoff Andrew, British Film Institute
Edward Buscombe
William Germano, The Cooper Union for the Advancement of Science and Art
Lalitha Gopalan, University of Texas at Austin
Lee Grieveson, University College London
Nick James, Editor, Sight & Sound

Laura Mulvey, Birkbeck College, University of London
Alastair Phillips, University of Warwick
Dana Polan, New York University
B. Ruby Rich, University of California, Santa Cruz
Amy Villarejo, Cornell University

The Birth of a Nation

Paul McEwan

 palgrave

A BFI book published by Palgrave

LIBRARY
NORTHERN VIRGINIA COMMUNITY COLLEGE

© Paul McEwan 2015

All rights reserved. No reproduction, copy or transmission of this publication may be made without written permission. No portion of this publication may be reproduced, copied or transmitted save with written permission or in accordance with the provisions of the Copyright, Designs and Patents Act 1988, or under the terms of any licence permitting limited copying issued by the Copyright Licensing Agency, Saffron House, 6–10 Kirby Street, London EC1N 8TS. Any person who does any unauthorised act in relation to this publication may be liable to criminal prosecution and civil claims for damages.

The author has asserted his right to be identified as the author of this work in accordance with the Copyright, Designs and Patents Act 1988.

First published in 2015 by
PALGRAVE

on behalf of the

BRITISH FILM INSTITUTE
21 Stephen Street, London W1T 1LN
www.bfi.org.uk

There's more to discover about film and television through the BFI. Our world-renowned archive, cinemas, festivals, films, publications and learning resources are here to inspire you.

Palgrave in the UK is an imprint of Macmillan Publishers Limited, registered in England, company number 785998, of 4 Crinan Street, London N1 9XW. Palgrave Macmillan in the US is a division of St Martin's Press LLC, 175 Fifth Avenue, New York, NY 10010. Palgrave is a global imprint of the above companies and is represented throughout the world. Palgrave® and Macmillan® are registered trademarks in the United States, the United Kingdom, Europe and other countries.

Series cover design: Ashley Western
Series text design: ketchup/SE14
Images from *The Birth of a Nation* (D. W. Griffith, 1915), © David W. Griffith Corporation/Epoch Producing Corporation

Set by Cambrian Typesetters, Camberley, Surrey
Printed in China

This book is printed on paper suitable for recycling and made from fully managed and sustained forest sources. Logging, pulping and manufacturing processes are expected to conform to the environmental regulations of the country of origin.

British Library Cataloguing-in-Publication Data
A catalogue record for this book is available from the British Library
A catalog record for this book is available from the Library of Congress

ISBN 978-1-84457-657-9

Contents

Acknowledgments   6

Introduction: 'True as That Blade'   7

1 The Film   16

2 The Legacy   80

Notes   92

Credits   99

Acknowledgments

This book would not exist in its present form without the extensive feedback of my students at Muhlenberg College, who have tolerated my over-interest in the film for a number of years, and whose thoughtfulness has repeatedly shaped my ideas and the book's content. I am grateful to my Film History class of 2014, who read the manuscript, and particularly indebted to Katrina Faust and Francesca Fillis, who were patient and thorough proofreaders. I am also thankful to my colleague Roberta Meek for useful advice about the book's design and perspective, and to Philippa Hudson for making innumerable improvements to the text. Sophie Contento from BFI/Palgrave was helpful from the proposal stage to final edits. Clearance for image rights was graciously supported by the Daniel J. and Carol Shiner Wilson Grant for the Completion of Scholarly Projects at Muhlenberg College.

Most of this book was written while on a research sabbatical from Muhlenberg in the fall of 2013, and I owe much to my colleagues, who have helped me carve out a place for writing and research amidst the daily pressures of working in a vibrant liberal arts college. My wife Eileen was my first editor and my sounding board. She and my children Grace and Max are a constant source of inspiration, as is my sister Nichola, a teacher and a crusader, to whom this book is dedicated.

Introduction: 'True as That Blade'

In an introduction to *The Birth of a Nation* that was shot for the film's re-release in 1930, D. W. Griffith sits for an awkward staged interview with the actor Walter Huston, who had recently starred in Griffith's *Abraham Lincoln* (1930). Huston gives Griffith a Confederate battle sword as a gift, and they discuss Griffith's most famous film. Huston asks Griffith if *The Birth of a Nation* is 'true', and Griffith initially replies 'true as that blade'. Upon reflection, though, he softens a bit and says, 'Yes, I think it's true … but as Pontius Pilate said, "Truth? What is the truth?" '

This is perhaps Griffith's most revealing moment in the history of his responses to *The Birth of a Nation*, and the only surviving public comment in which he expresses the slightest doubt that his film is anything less than the absolute historical truth. In 1915, he had written that it was 'based upon truth in every vital detail',[1] a somewhat bizarre claim given that it is a work of historical fiction in which most of the primary characters are either made up or only loosely based on real figures. *The Birth of a Nation* had been adapted from a novel by Thomas Dixon, first published in 1905, and a subsequent stage play.

To modern viewers, *The Birth of a Nation* is sometimes incomprehensible. We expect that films created in the past will include stereotypical images of minorities, but a film in which the Ku Klux Klan are the heroes becomes more shocking with every passing decade. Many first-time viewers, especially younger ones, have trouble believing that such a film was ever made, let alone that it was incredibly popular.[2]

Assessing the historical legacy of *The Birth of a Nation* requires grappling with a complex calculus of racism and art, a mixture that has created arguments and confounded viewers for the past century.

The Birth of a Nation is, in the simplest terms, one of our culture's greatest artistic achievements and one of its most racist artefacts. Our temptation has long been to try to combine these two ideas by arithmetic in an attempt to determine whether the net result is positive or negative, or whether one simply cancels out the other. For much of its history, the impossibility of reconciling these two conflicting ideals has led otherwise well-intentioned people to simply ignore the racism, to try to set it aside so that they can consider the film as art unencumbered.

The core of the dilemma is that we often think of art as beautiful and noble, something to be admired and respected, something that uplifts society, even if it deals with difficult topics. There is little place in our understanding of art for a film that exalts ideals we now find repulsive, and there are very few historical works that fall into this category. *The Birth of a Nation*'s closest peers in this difficult territory are the Nazi films of Leni Riefenstahl,

In a filmed introduction to the 1930 re-release of the film with a soundtrack, actor Walter Huston (left) presents D. W. Griffith with the sword of a Confederate officer

particularly *The Triumph of the Will* (1935). In filmic terms, *The Triumph of the Will* has little in common with *The Birth of a Nation*. As a documentary, it is less constructed around a dramatic climax, and its scenes of massive rallies are disturbing because we know why those crowds are cheering. In other contexts, we might see such assemblies as patriotic displays or evidence of democracy in action.[3] The fact that *The Triumph of the Will* is structured around large crowds rather than individual protagonists makes it easier for modern audiences to keep their distance from its ideology.

By the same token, many films since *The Birth of a Nation* have featured a dramatic race-to-the-rescue of one type or another, often with cross-cutting between rescuer and potential victim, a technique that Griffith had helped to pioneer in his earlier films. But in this case, even viewers horrified by the film and by the Klan can perhaps, momentarily, find themselves caught up in the excitement of the rides to save Elsie Stoneman and then the people in the cabin, who are in apparent mortal danger. The Klan's ride to the rescue, with its moving camera and overpowering score, is a central exhibit in Hollywood cinema's ability to elevate emotions over critical thinking.

To point out that the final scenes of *The Birth of a Nation* are compelling examples of narrative power is not to excuse the content or to sidestep it. Rather, acknowledgment of the film's power allows us to confront its ideology directly. By admitting that the film is well done, we can better understand its power over audiences. If *The Birth of a Nation* had been a poorly made film that valorised the Klan, it would have been quickly forgotten and perhaps lost – at best it

Birth of a Nation advertisement in a Chicago newspaper, January 1916

would be a minor historical curiosity. The film's power comes from the fact that it succeeds in making the audiences identify with the protagonists, even when they do not share those protagonists' views.

The art-or-racism argument that has followed *The Birth of a Nation* since its release is clearly a false choice. It is both art and racist, and the fact that it is art does not excuse or mitigate the racism. The inverse proposition is more complicated – does the fact that it is racist mitigate its status as a work of art?

The notion of art as inherently beautiful and reflective of humankind's finer nature has a long history, but it is a notion that has taken a critical beating in the last forty years, in a theoretical landscape that has played down the distinction between high and low culture in favour of seeing various works as simply reflections of culture. Scholars tend to eschew discussion of good or bad art, other than when talking about how *other people* view that art. In such a postmodern critical framework, *The Birth of a Nation* is easier to place: art is a reflection of culture. Racist cultures will have racist works of art. *The Birth of a Nation* is thus a racist work of art made in a racist culture.

The catch is that academic criticism is nowhere near as postmodern as it likes to pretend. As much as we try to avoid discussions of artistic canons, such evaluations are inherent in the choices of university syllabi and publishers' book lists. While film studies has a much broader scope than some fields when it comes to considering objects worth of study, a few objects are still outside of that scope – for example, many contemporary Hollywood films that are neither artistic nor historic. When we write about films, it is clear that some are interesting for sociological and historical reasons rather than because we consider them 'art'. Some films get the auteur treatment and others do not, depending on whether we are trying to elevate them. Even in the cases of films considered artistic masterpieces like *Citizen Kane* (1941), we do not write about them in the way literature scholars write about *Hamlet*, or even *Moby Dick*. There are no essays that focus exclusively on minor characters in *Citizen Kane*, and no journals of Welles Studies.

All of this is to say that for better or worse, we cling to what are supposed to be old-fashioned and romantic notions about the nature of art, which is why discussions about *The Birth of a Nation* still carry so much bite. Talking about the film's artistic achievements and influences sounds inherently like we are justifying or excusing its moral failings, because art is supposed to be a force for good. The higher our emotional and intellectual stakes in the notion of art, the more difficult the balancing act becomes. The appeal of the postmodern position is that we sidestep this act. If we can only give up our romantic notions about art, things become much easier. But what a thing to give up completely. Better instead, I would argue, to grapple with our conundrum forcefully, with the goal not of wrestling one side or the other into submission but of living with the deeply troubling ambiguity. It is not the film that is morally ambiguous, but our response to it. Learning to live with the conundrum that *The Birth of a Nation* presents allows us to better understand what it meant to Griffith when he made it and what it meant to the audiences who saw it. If we either dismiss it as a racist object or decide to talk about its use of close-ups, we only get a piece of the picture, whereas a cultural product as complicated as this must be considered from as many perspectives as possible to be understood.

As if the situation were not already complex enough, there is another angle that complicates our response further. On top of everything else, *The Birth of a Nation* was a singular historical event.

Colour flyer for 1930 re-release of the film

May 20, 1920   THE GREATER AMUSEMENTS   12

Now Booking

SECURE DATES NOW

THE GREATEST OF ALL

MASTERPIECE D. W. GRIFFITH'S MASTERPIECE
8TH WONDER OF THE WORLD

5000
SCENES

THE **BIRTH** OF A **NATION**

1800
PEOPLE

COST
$500,000

3000
HORSES

BIG AS EVER

WITH ORIGINAL BIG ORCHESTRA
AND
THE OLD TIME CIRCUS BILLING IN ADVANCE

Just Played Miner Theatre, St. Cloud, Minn. Three Days to S. R. O.
Oh' Yes it Will Repeat. Only 6 Times in St. Cloud Before

ELLIOTT FILM CORPORATION
507 Produce Exchange Building   MINNEAPOLIS, MINN.

It was not the first feature film, nor even the first historical epic, but it helped to ensconce the feature film as the dominant mode of Hollywood film-making and solidified many of the film-making codes that exist to this day. The film's length alone made it remarkable – about three hours, at a time when features were often less than half that length and many films were still one- or two-reelers. The budget was much bigger than had been typical, as was the time and effort that went into making the film.[4] Indeed, it was the film's ambition that set it apart. In an environment of short genre films made with low budgets, this was an attempt at telling a complex historical story with multiple protagonists and plotlines, using individual stories to encourage audience identification with characters distant from them. It tried to elevate the status of film by playing in legitimate theatres for high ticket prices, accompanied by a live orchestra and a specially composed score. Griffith tried to change many of the rules of film presentation all at once, and managed to succeed on nearly every level that mattered to him. The film was both critically well-received and immensely popular. It created a narrative structure and form recognisable in nearly every other historical epic that Hollywood has produced since.

Thus, *The Birth of a Nation* lies not just at the intersection of art and race, but also at the intersection of art and race and cinema history.[5] Had it been a similar commercial and artistic success, but made ten years later, we would probably not pay it the same attention, since it would not be such a cinematic milestone and we

Trade advertisement in *The Greater Amusements* for a re-release of *The Birth of a Nation* in 1920

could choose to ignore it if we preferred. The fact that it is such a key text in the history of cinema's development means that we have not had the luxury of leaving it aside, even when we were poorly equipped to deal with its complexity. At every point in the development of film culture over the past hundred years, film partisans and scholars have had to confront this text because it sits in the centre of the field, forcing us to acknowledge its presence whether we like it or not. At the founding of the Museum of Modern Art's film library in 1935, or among the hundreds of amateur cinema clubs that sprang up in the middle of the century, or in the halls of universities where film studies tried to establish itself in the 1960s and 70s as a worthy field of study, *The Birth of a Nation* was the troublesome film that had to be confronted.

As a nascent medium whose status as art was not taken for granted or in any way guaranteed, film was an art form not only in need of art and artists, but in need of an artistic history. At key points in the formation of this history – at MoMA, in film clubs and in the academy – *The Birth of a Nation* had to be wrestled with. In some cases, this history is remarkable for the sophistication with which film critics and fans weighed the film's attributes and weaknesses. In other cases, the record is less admirable, as there was a tendency to simply ignore or set aside the racism of the film to focus on its form and history. This was particularly the case in universities from the 1960s on, where the film was often taught defensively or obliviously. Perhaps because the status of film studies in the academy was genuinely precarious, the emphasis tended to be on historical artistic masterpieces over readings that confronted race. It seems likely that the sharp racial polarisation of the era made the film's portrayals of African Americans difficult to talk about, especially for scholars who had no expertise in doing so. They knew film and film history, so for the most part that is where they concentrated their attention.

Our default habit is to examine historical films in the light of our own epoch, our own ideologies and our own biases. This is especially complicated in the case of *The Birth of a Nation*, since there are very few cultural objects whose cultural reception has shifted so completely over time. Clearly, my discussion of the film's racism thus far benefits from the passing of a century, when the hard-fought (and hard-thought) developments of civil rights have become the moral foundations of much of our culture. Some might reply that it is unfair to apply the moral codes of the early twenty-first century to the culture of the early twentieth. This argument is partially correct, but is also insufficient for a number of reasons. The first is historical – there were plenty of people who pointed out the racism of *The Birth of a Nation* when it was released, and who made their case in rhetorical and moral terms nearly indistinguishable from the way we talk about civil rights now.[6] The proportion of the film's audience that took issue with the film was far smaller than it would be today, but it was sizeable enough to stimulate a loud and vociferous public debate, and for Griffith to feel compelled to respond. It is often remarked that Griffith's next film, *Intolerance* (1916), was a response to the criticism he received over *The Birth of a Nation*, and this is true in part, but not in the way that modern audiences might perceive – it was in no way an apology. *Intolerance* tells four thematically linked stories: the fall of ancient Babylon, the crucifixion of Jesus Christ, the persecution of the French Huguenots in the sixteenth century and a modern-day story of a young man wrongly accused of murder. In each of the stories, the moral is that human intolerance of those who differ has always been a scourge on humanity. Modern audiences would easily read racism into that list of harmful intolerances, which is why *Intolerance* can seem like an apology for *The Birth of a Nation*. It is not. Griffith made clear in numerous public statements that he had nothing to apologise for in regard to *The Birth of a Nation*, and that *Intolerance* was intended as a commentary on those who had been intolerant of *him*.[7]

The argument that we should not condemn Griffith from our modern moral viewpoint is superficially true. We must remember, individually, not to claim some sort of inherent superiority over Griffith or anyone else of his era. This is not the same thing as failing to condemn the belief itself. We can, and should, assert that our modern belief in racial equality is morally superior to the racist beliefs that we are struggling to leave behind, but should do so without inverting cause and effect. Believing in racial equality *makes us* better people; we do not believe in it *because* we are better people.

The phrase popularised by Martin Luther King Jr, that 'the arc of the moral universe is long, but it bends towards justice', was likely written by Theodore Parker, a nineteenth-century abolitionist. Parker's version includes the limitation that 'my eye reaches but little ways'. This reminds us that our own present perspective is limited, and that we should be humble about how well we can see.

With this in mind, we must do our best to consider *The Birth of a Nation* in the artistic, industrial and moral environment in which it was created. It is a difficult and compelling task, one that reminds us how far we have come, and how far we have yet to go.

1 The Film

Given how much would eventually be written about the film,[8] the review of *The Birth of a Nation* in *The New York Times* on 4 March 1915, the day after its debut in the city, is remarkably succinct.[9] Nevertheless, in fewer than three hundred words, the unsigned review manages to cover much that will be debated for the next century. Allowing that the film has an 'ambitious scale', the reviewer describes it as 'a film version of some of the melodramatic and inflammatory material contained in "The Clansman," by Thomas Dixon', and remarks that 'A great deal might be said concerning the spirit revealed in Mr Dixon's review of the unhappy chapter of Reconstruction and concerning the sorry service rendered by its plucking at old wounds.'

The Birth of a Nation claims to be an accurate history of the Civil War and the period immediately afterwards, commonly known as the Reconstruction. It was made fifty years after the war and attempted to tell a story about the country's darkest days, with the goal of unifying the nation and underscoring commonality rather than division. One hundred years later, it is of little use to us as a history of the Civil War or Reconstruction, but tells us a great deal about the time in which it was made. To modern eyes, it cannot be a unifying story, because its assumptions are so fundamentally racist. Griffith often argued that his film was not racist at all and was simply a true depiction of a difficult period in history, but the racism of the era in which he lived and worked was so deep, so endemic and so unremarkable to the vast majority of citizens that it was indeed invisible.

This is clear in the first proper intertitle of the film, which follows the titles and the defences of the motion picture: 'The bringing of the African to America planted the first seed of disunion.' The intertitle,

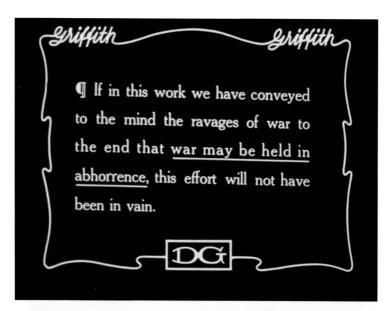

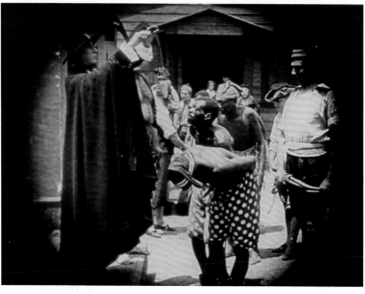

Title card from the beginning of the film; title: 'The bringing of the African to America planted the first seed of disunion'

and the quick shot that follows of a man in Puritan-style clothing raising his hands over a bound slave, makes it clear that the presence of African slaves in the United States was a problem because of the division it created among the white people of the country. *The Birth of a Nation*, despite its length and complexity, is fundamentally a story about brothers and sisters torn asunder who are reunited at the end. The entirety of the film leads towards the resolution of this narrative arc, when, under attack in the cabin, the partisans of North and South put their differences aside 'in defence of their common Aryan birthright'. At the outset, the film introduces the 'seeds of disunion' that will fuel the conflict, but in terms of narrative function these seeds could just as well be something else – money or land or anything that causes a rift in a family. In this story, Africans are regarded as objects over which 'people' will fight, rather than as people in their own right with worthy desires or needs. For most of the film, the needs of the slaves or former slaves are limited to whatever can be conveniently provided by white overseers. Indeed, the only 'positive' portrayals of non-white characters in the film – the only ones who are not schemers or fools or racists – are the Camerons' loyal servants, who defend their masters selflessly and attack less deferential blacks with what is supposed to be admirable fervour. Griffith used these characters to defend himself from attacks, writing that:

we do pay particular attention to those faithful Negroes who stayed with their former masters and were ready to give up their lives to protect their white friends. No characters in the story are applauded with greater fervor than the good Negroes whose devotion is so clearly shown. If prejudiced witnesses do not see the message in this portion of the entire drama we are not to blame.[10]

The title about the bringing of Africans to America also establishes a second notable feature of *The Birth of a Nation* – the forcefulness of its written narrative voice. The practice of writing

intertitles varied greatly in the silent era, but for the most part the
idea was to include as few as possible, which means that in general
these titles are limited to dialogue and any necessary information that
is not clearly conveyed by the images. Because *The Birth of a Nation*
pushed the boundaries of narrative complexity in 1915, it is more
dependent on intertitles than many silent films. Whatever else
modern viewers might think about the film, it is not very difficult to
follow, something that cannot be said about many other films of the
period, including Griffith's own *Intolerance*.

   The titles in *The Birth of a Nation* contain a strong narrative
voice that directs the viewer's attention and tells him or her what to
think about the scenes that follow. The power of this voice is clear if
we imagine rewriting many of the titles that belabour the villainy of
the northern carpetbaggers and the noble virtues of the racists.
It could never be a story about racial equality or understanding,
since the racism is also so deeply embodied in the performances of

Griffith's 'faithful negroes': Mammy defends Dr Cameron from mockery white actors wearing blackface makeup, but its most extreme rhetoric could be greatly mitigated. In fact, the 1930 re-release of the film does exactly that at key moments – its intertitles are almost completely rewritten. The vast majority of the new titles simply rephrase the original content, but there are important modifications, including the title near the end about the 'Aryan birthright', which was changed to declare simply that the two sides were united against 'the carpetbaggers' mad folly'. Throughout the dramatically shortened (under two hours) 1930 re-release, which is the version many viewers saw for the next fifty years, the racist rhetoric is toned down and the film reads as much more of an action-adventure story and less of an epic history.[11]

Attention to the titles reminds us that much of the power of *The Birth of a Nation* lies in the interplay between what we see and what we read. If the common advice to novice writers and film-makers alike is to show rather than tell, *The Birth of a Nation* is a film that both shows and tells. As such, it is a key link between written and filmic storytelling, and a film that tries to maintain the historical authority of the written word while providing audiences with the thrill of visual immersion. This tension between written authority and the freedom of storytelling has played out in historical epic films up to the present day, although in nearly all subsequent cases the written authority becomes extra-textual, a part of the public relations campaigns for historical films advertising the attention to historical detail in the *mise en scène*, the amount of work that has gone into period costuming, or the attestations of experts or witnesses that a film is an accurate representation of its subject matter. Such extra-textual evidence surrounds films like *Saving Private Ryan* (1998), *JFK* (1991) or *12 Years a Slave* (2013). In the case of *The Birth of a Nation*, it is also written directly into the film itself. Eager for it to be taken seriously as a work of history, Griffith included citations of written works throughout the film, arguing in one interview that in libraries of the future, rather than reading about history, patrons might be able to press a button and actually *see* what happened in a particular period.[12]

¶ Appomattox Courthouse, on the afternoon of April 9, 1865, the surrender of Gen. Robt. E. Lee, C. S. A., to Gen. U. S. Grant, U. S. A.

AN HISTORICAL FACSIMILE of the Wilmer McLean home as on that occasion, and the principals and their staffs, after Col. Horace Porter in "Campaigning with Grant."

Such film boosterism misses the obvious fact that these library films would be subject to all of the same biases as written works, and also that narrative films are generally terrible at conveying the nuances of evidence in the way that historical writing can. Ideally, historical writing can clearly outline the evidence that exists for a particular idea or event, and rhetorically mark its own doubts and misgivings.[13] Film cannot do any of these things without breaking continuity – within a scene, there is no way to indicate which lines of dialogue are part of the historical record and which are invented, or to convey the idea that evidence for an event is contradictory. This is why historical fiction films often try to coat themselves in a general sheen of historical accuracy by publicising the names of the veterans who were present for the filming of certain scenes or the research that went into the construction of sets. Such manoeuvres are the filmic equivalent of a book that contains a bibliography but no footnotes, providing assurance that research went into the production but eliding

Title card with footnote

To the Honorable, The Department of
Education of Ohio, Division of
Film Censorship

Application

of Epoch Producing Corporation of
New York City, N. Y., in behalf
of Film entitled

The Birth of a
Nation

ᔕᕗ

CHAS. SUMNER DRUGGAN and
CHAS. J. TRAINOR,
Attorneys for Applicant,

any discussion of the particulars and making it impossible for audiences to selectively evaluate the evidence.

The Birth of a Nation uses this confusion about evidence to great advantage, purposely blurring the line between what can be referenced and what is invented. The film is, of course, based on a novel and stage play rather than works of historical non-fiction, but it is important to note that, even if the core story is invented, the vast majority of historical works on the Reconstruction available in 1915 would have agreed with Griffith's version of history. The prominence of what came to be known as the Dunning School (after William A. Dunning of Columbia University[14]) meant that Griffith and his lawyers could defend their film against charges of racism by referencing written academic histories. Griffith's attorneys eventually produced an annotated bibliography for the film that was used in a court case in Ohio.[15]

The written references within *The Birth of a Nation* – to the biography of Lincoln by John George Nicolay and John Milton Hay,[16] or to Woodrow Wilson's *A History of the American People* – give the film a general sense of historical accuracy that carries over into other details, as in the scene on the Camerons' plantation, where the title reads: 'In the slave quarters. The two-hour interval given for dinner, out of their working day from six till six.' Including such specific detail about working hours suggests careful research and is thus less likely to be questioned. Such rhetoric makes slavery sound

Cover page for a collection of testimonials about the film to be used in an appeal to the Ohio state censor board, February 1925

reasonable, and indeed we see shots of slaves working contentedly and even dancing, rather than scenes of the physical violence upon which the institution depended. Slavery, of course, only provides a background to the story of the Camerons and the Stonemans, and it is the narrative form, rather than specific claims about slave life, that most convinces the viewer to align their sympathies with the slave owners rather than with the slaves themselves.

In his study of Griffith's work in 1908 and 1909, Tom Gunning traces the development of the director's film-making style, and argues that it is narrative that defines Griffith rather than individual camera shots or editing. As much as Griffith claimed credit for many formal advances, these had been invented by others. Gunning argues that:

What is missing in these earlier filmmakers, although it appears at points in their work, is an unambiguous subordination of filmic discourse to narrative purposes. Under Griffith, the devices of cinema that were generally displayed

Slaves dance for their masters

for their own sake as attractions in the work of earlier filmmakers became channeled toward the expression of characterization and story. The often free-floating filmic attractions of early film became part of a narrative system as film unambiguously defined its primary role as a teller of tales, a constructor of narratives.[17]

There are many moments early on in *The Birth of a Nation* that demonstrate the sophistication of Griffith's technique, which he had further developed between 1909 and 1915. The early shots of slavery and of abolitionist meetings are efficient and summative, but once we move into the primary story, characters are introduced quickly but carefully. We first meet the Camerons as Ben walks along the street, chats politely with a woman in a carriage and plays with his younger sister. The father sits calmly, and his peaceful character is both stated plainly in the intertitles and then demonstrated in the action, as he plays with puppies and kittens. The sister Margaret appears, and we now have a picture of a close-knit family, which also includes a loyal

Ben Cameron and an unnamed young woman in a carriage

slave fixing the young girl's hair (like all the primary black and mixed-race characters in the film, this character is played by a white actor in blackface).

In the space of several minutes, we meet the entire family and the story gradually moves forward as the Stonemans arrive from the north and the multiple relationships begin to develop. The younger sons from each family horse around with each other, calling attention to their age, while the first of the romantic relationships is hinted at, between Margaret Cameron and Phil Stoneman. The friendship between the boys will soon become crucial, when they meet on a Civil War battlefield on opposite sides of the conflict, and the poignancy of that melodrama is set up at their first meeting by this image, as they act more like children than grown men.

At this point in his career, Griffith knew how to construct a scene, and the editing is remarkably modern. Shots are cut on entrances and exits with little lag, and the spatial relations of the

The youngest boys meet

front of the house (following what is now called the 180-degree rule) are clear. It differs very little from modern film-making techniques, with one significant exception in some versions.

In most modern cuts of *The Birth of a Nation*, which are generally descended from 1921 prints with additions from a range of sources,[18] the character of Margaret Cameron is inserted almost at random into the scene. As Ben Cameron walks up the street and stops to talk to the woman in the carriage, a title is inserted into the shot that reads, 'Margaret Cameron, a daughter of the South, trained in the manners of the old school.' While the placement of the title infers that Margaret is the woman in the carriage, the next shot shows the actual Margaret Cameron walking around inside the house, picking up an umbrella and putting it down. The scene then cuts back to Ben talking to the unidentified woman in the carriage. The insertion of the title card and shot of Margaret at this point makes no sense whatsoever, and the confusion continues when other shots of Margaret are inserted at intervals in the scene. Following the shot of puppies in a basket, we see her descend the stairs inside the house, and then, after a kitten is dropped onto the puppies (labelled 'Hostilities'), Margaret finds a letter on the hall table and excitedly brings it out to Ben. It is the letter announcing the arrival of their northern cousins, and from here the action moves forward conventionally.

It is impossible to know if these seemingly random shots of Margaret Cameron are part of Griffith's original vision of the scene, or an artefact of filmic reconstruction. We do know that in the 1930 re-release, the scene is 'fixed', so that the title card announcing Margaret appears just before she comes out of the house with the letter, and the shot of Ben talking to the woman in the carriage is not interrupted. Given the complicated history of the existing versions, it is possible that this 'fixed' version is actually in line with the original, and that the interrupted version has some other origins. In at least some re-release prints, though, there is clearly a slight jump where the earlier version cuts to Margaret, implying that the shot had been there but was removed in 1930.

There are at least two other interesting differences in the construction of this scene in the 1930 re-release. In the earlier version, as Ben Cameron walks up the street, a horse-drawn cart carrying slaves pulls away from the kerb, and two children fall off the back. A man picks them up and spanks one of them over his knee. In the 1930 version, the shot has been replaced by an alternative take in which only one child falls off the cart, and although the man picks up the child roughly, he does not spank him with the stick. Also, the letter from the northern cousins is different in the 1930 version – framed in iris, it looks much more like it could have been shot in 1914 than the letter in the 'standard' version, which has no iris and does not match the colour tone of the scene. This difference is true of all the letters in the 1930 version.

We cannot say with certainty which of the letters, alternative takes or editing sequences are original, and in the case of Griffith the notion of 'original' is deeply misleading, carrying with it a sense of the 'real' film that is impossible to achieve.[19] It is entirely possible that the nonsensical insertion of Margaret Cameron in most modern prints is the mark of a hand other than Griffith's, but it is also possibly his own, revised by him or others later. We know that he edited the film substantially after it was released, but also that individual prints would have been handled by many others – censors, theatre owners and those who have reconstructed the film over the years.

It is worth recounting these differences at length to remind ourselves of the contingencies inherent in making specific claims about the form of films from the silent era, but also to draw attention to the fact that in the case of *The Birth of a Nation*, it is not these small choices that are so remarkable. Rather, it is the overall narrative construction of the film – the fact that Griffith is able to set the historical scene with a few short sequences, introduce a plethora of characters, establish their basic personalities and relationships, and insert them plausibly into the sweep of history, and do it all within the first hour or so of the film.

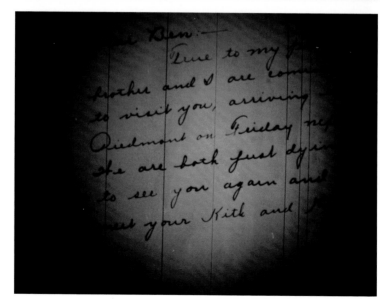

Letter in 'standard version' of film (dating from 1921); letter in 1930 re-release version

This combination of individual character development and historical sweep has been central to the historical epic ever since, and is clearly recognisable in much later blockbusters like *Titanic* (1997). These films typically use individuals to make historical conflicts personal and build our sympathies, so that we will be more attuned to large-scale tragedy. Vivian Sobchack has written that the mode of address in historical films is built on the 'projection of *ourselves-now* to *we-then*', which she contrasts to the more distanced mode of formal historical writing, which is built on the 'projection of *ourselves-now* as *others-then*'.[20] Such a distinction is crucial to understanding the appeal of historical drama, and its limitations. Sobchack uses the distinction in the context of arguments about historical truth in film to argue that 'neither mode of historicizing, of creating History, is "truer" than the other'.[21] It seems much more useful to point out that the filmic mode has dramatic and even educational advantages, while acknowledging that a lot of facts tend to be sacrificed along the way. There is a benefit to being able to *feel* a sense of the past that often requires a glossing over of details.

This trade-off is not specific to film, of course. It is a feature of historical fiction and of stage plays, and thus not an invention of Griffith's. Once again, Griffith is the amalgamator, gathering a set of practices from his own films, from the films of others, from fiction, from the stage (where he began his career as an actor) and from history books. It is the marriage of a pre-existing convention (individual stories against a historical backdrop) and the still developing codes of cinematography, *mise en scène* and editing that makes *The Birth of a Nation* a milestone. What is strangest about the film now is how not-strange it is – how many of its conventions have barely evolved in a century. It can be difficult to see past the lens of the Klan, but we can be grateful that it is the film's narrative structure that has survived the century rather than its politics, especially since there was hardly a guarantee in 1915 that film would survive the century at all.

The first major dramatic scene in the North is the meeting between Austin Stoneman and Charles Sumner, leader of the Senate. The discussion between the two men is simply a set-up for the real action, which takes place outside the office between Sumner and Lydia, Stoneman's 'mulatto' housekeeper. As Sumner asks for his hat, Lydia pointedly drops it on the floor. After he leaves, Lydia has the idea of pretending that Sumner has attacked her, and tears her own dress. Before Stoneman enters, a title card announces, 'The great leader's weakness, that is to blight a nation.' He finds Lydia in tears and comforts her, but is tempted by her bare shoulder, which he caresses. She pulls away, and as he embraces her again from behind, the film cuts to the next scene.

This interaction between Stoneman and Lydia was one of the most frequently censored scenes, so much so that it has been missing in most recent prints.[22] The censors' concern was about the portrayal of interracial romance, which seems somewhat misguided

A frequently censored shot in which Stoneman touches the shoulder of his maid Lydia

given that the film is unambiguously opposed to miscegenation. This invective is clearly embodied in Lydia herself, as well as in the person of Silas Lynch, who imposes Stoneman's will on the South and eventually tries to force a marriage with Stoneman's daughter Elsie. In the middle of the film, immediately after the death of Abraham Lincoln, Stoneman and Lydia embrace once more, at which point she tells him that he is now 'the greatest power in America' and grasps his arm. Although it suggests a romantic relationship, the moment is much less sexual in tone.

In a film full of ugly stereotypes, the mixed-race characters are presented as unrelenting schemers and villains who refuse to occupy their proper place on the lower rungs of society. The novel and stage version of *The Clansman* (Thomas Dixon's play on which *The Birth of a Nation* is based) make clear that miscegenation is the greatest fear of white supremacists, because it blurs the categories upon which their worldview depends. In one rebuttal of a *Birth of a Nation* critic published in *The New York Globe*, Griffith argued that some of the film's critics had spoken in favour of intermarriage between blacks and whites, and this was obviously intended to be a devastating dismissal of the critic's views.[23] Preventing miscegenation was clearly one of Dixon's reasons for being and while it does not seem to have been one of Griffith's, the idea of interracial marriage was obviously repugnant to him, as it would have been to many white Americans in 1915. The last laws banning interracial marriage in the United States were only overturned in 1967, and even then by Supreme Court order rather than by direct democracy.[24]

The American system of racial repression depended in part on an overhyped fear of black men attacking white women. While this was extremely rare, the fear provided a convenient excuse to keep both groups under tight control. It was, of course, much more common for white men to take advantage of black women, especially of the slaves under their supervision. The well-publicised case of Thomas Jefferson and Sally Hemings is perhaps the best-known account of a white man fathering children with an enslaved

woman.[25] In the case of *The Birth of a Nation*, it is indeed a white man who attempts to have a relationship with his mulatto servant. To Dixon, this represented a pollution of the white ideal, and obviously the character of Lydia is doubly marked, since her existence means that miscegenation has already taken place.

The reference to Stoneman's 'weakness' is a condemnation, but one that, in the context of the film, sees him as a victim of the scheming Lydia, who has torn her own dress in an attempt to win his sympathy and his romantic attentions. This is a crucial subplot, since part of the narrative resolution at the end of the film will be Stoneman's horror when he realises that Silas Lynch wants to marry his daughter Elsie. Stoneman is a supporter of interracial marriage, and the fact that he recoils when Lynch suggests marrying Elsie is supposed to represent his realisation of the error of his ways – a case of the political becoming personal that puts him on the 'correct' path to a recognition of white supremacy.

Lydia schemes

In the first half of the film, miscegenation and race are background to the story of the Civil War and the idea of friends divided, but in a scene of Piedmont being 'scarred by the war', Griffith cannot help using one of his footnotes to mention that 'The first negro regiments of the war were raised in South Carolina.' There is no citation for this fact (which is largely true, depending on whether or not we are talking about official regiments[26]), but pointing it out implies that someone should have foreseen what trouble it would cause. Black regiments did not exist until the middle of the war, because of fears in the North about how armed black soldiers would behave, and about black and white soldiers serving side by side. As the war dragged on, the first of these fears was overcome, but blacks served in segregated units supervised by white officers.[27]

This title card was dramatically rewritten for the 1930 version of the film, to read: 'Piedmont suffers a guerrilla raid. Viciousness, brought forth by war, is common to all races.' This is a remarkable switch in meaning given that neither Griffith nor anyone associated with the film had ever offered any apology or correction. The change may reflect the hand of producers Roy and Harry Aitken, who recut the film.[28] In the scene itself, one that uses African-American actors to play the troops, soldiers run amok throughout the town and into the Cameron household. In the streets, white men are shot on sight and a black woman dances around the body of an elderly white man who has just been shot. The raid continues until a unit of Confederate soldiers rides to the rescue. The melodrama kicks into high gear in the following scene, in which the two youngest sons of the Camerons and Stonemans meet face to face on the battlefield and die dramatically in each other's arms. This, and the scenes of mourning by both families that follow, cement the reading of the film as a story of divided families in which the commonalities outweigh the divisions.

As the war develops on screen, Griffith is at his strongest. In a much celebrated iris shot of a mother and children huddled on a

A guerrilla raid on Piedmont: black soldiers and civilians in the foreground laugh over the body of a white man who has just been shot; the youngest boys meet again on the battlefield

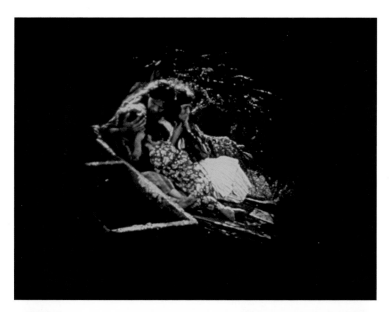

A shot of a family huddled on a hilltop pans to a view of the battlefield below

hilltop, the camera pans right and slowly opens up to reveal armies on the battlefield far below. This blend of medium and long shots was innovative, incorporating the small- and large-scale elements of the war into a single shot. A similar effect is created a few shots later without the moving camera, when soldiers and the wounded fleeing Atlanta pull themselves towards the camera through a gap in a fence. These figures are framed at the bottom of the image, and we can see above them a long line of people stretching off into the distance, while being close enough to the characters in the foreground to read their agonised expressions. We cut to a chaotic Atlanta street scene, which provides a pointed contrast with the earlier shots of Piedmont celebrating on the eve of the war. Since the Piedmont revellers were carrying fireworks, that scene was also full of fire and smoke, and both sequences are tinted red in some prints. The Atlanta street scenes are followed by a trick shot. We see the people streaming through the fence again, but a close look reveals it to be the same actors repeating their actions on a different take. In this second sequence, however, the upper right corner of the frame is filled with a picture of Atlanta in flames. So, in a series of just a few shots, Griffith includes contrasts of scale, expert moving shots, visual contrasts to earlier scenes, trick shots and an 'efficient' use of crowd scenes, all with the cumulative effect of forcefully conveying the horrors of war.

Immediately afterwards, we have the brief scene of the death of Wade, the second Cameron son, on the field of battle. As he falls back and looks skywards, the film cuts to another battle scene, but one in which the image is initially completely obscured by smoke, creating the fleeting impression that it depicts Wade's heavenward gaze. When the fog clears, we are in the thick of battle again, and the effect of this blurring is similar to the one Francis Ford Coppola and his sound designer Walter Murch created decades later in *Apocalypse Now* (1979), when Willard lies in his hotel bed and the sound of helicopters mixes with the whirring of his ceiling fan – our confusion mirrors the characters', and the mental

anguishes of war are conveyed not just with *mise en scène*, but with editing and cinematography.

The next two sequences in the film are among Griffith's most masterful and the clearest demonstration of his techniques. Both scenes have significant racist content in Dixon's novel, but it has been erased by Griffith, making it possible for us to briefly imagine a different kind of film from the one we have. The sequences concern Ben Cameron's acts of bravery on the field of battle and his convalescence in the hospital afterwards. The battle scene is first framed in the most noble terms possible – the need to get a food train through to starving Confederate troops. Cameron, now 'The Little Colonel', is given the order to lead a charge against Union lines. What follows is a stunning collection of wide shots filmed from a hill in which the armies face each other across a no-man's-land with artillery smoke filling the air. Significant alternative footage of these scenes survives and has been restored by the Library of Congress, allowing us to see that Griffith filmed from many angles and chose the best shots later.[29]

As Cameron leads a charge across the screen from left to right, soldiers immediately begin to fall. Although the screen directions are maintained in general, there is no strict adherence to the 180-degree rule here – we sometimes cut to a medium shot of Cameron that is

Citizens flee the burning of Atlanta; the death of Wade Cameron filmed ever so slightly from the opposite side, so that he is running from the top of the screen to the bottom. The net effect is to give the scenes some sense of confusion while maintaining the basic relationships of the characters to one another. We also cut away at least twice to shots of the Cameron family at home, praying for the safety of their sons. The battle scenes are remarkably graphic. Opposing soldiers meet over barricades and begin to fight with bayonets and fists, while others try to strangle each other with their bare hands. One shot shows a Union soldier slowly stabbing two different Confederates with a bayonet.

Ben Cameron jumps across his own lines to give water to a dying Union soldier splayed in front of him, and we are told that 'The Unionists cheer the heroic deed.' As Cameron makes his last charge at the Union lines, he is hit in the final few feet and, in an image of high drama, manages to ram a flag into the mouth of a Union cannon. This incident appears in Dixon's novel, where the Union soldier recounting the tale adds that 'it's a sin to kill men like that. One such man is worth more to this nation than every negro that ever set his flat foot on this continent!'[30]

At moments such as this we can get a sense of Griffith's variance from Dixon. It is not simply that Griffith 'toned down' the racism in *The Birth of a Nation*, although for what it's worth, he certainly did. More than that, *The Birth of a Nation* and the novel and stage versions of *The Clansman* are narratives with different aims. Dixon's novel is a political tract written in the form of a novel, one whose primary aim is not to entertain but to warn the public about the spectre of miscegenation, which is why the discussions of race are inserted at every opportunity. In Griffith's case, the clear intent was to tell a story of peace and brotherhood, even if it was one built on a foundation of white supremacy.

To draw such a distinction between Dixon and Griffith is not to declare Griffith the lesser of two evils and let him off the hook. This has in fact been the manoeuvre adopted by numerous Griffith defenders over the years, as if claiming that a film is not as racist as it

While the battle rages, the Cameron family prays at home

A Confederate soldier being stabbed

Ben Cameron's symbolic victory on the battlefield

could have been is somehow a badge of honour. The distinction is important, however, because of what it says about Griffith's storytelling instincts. When Ben Cameron rams the battle flag into the enemy cannons, it is a flash of intense drama that would be undermined by the inclusion of the speech about him being 'worth more to this nation than every negro that ever set his flat foot on this continent'. Such a statement, with its evocative insult, would interrupt the flow of the scene and the emotion of Cameron's pyrrhic victory.

Late in the film, the title card about the cabin dwellers being 'united in defence of their Aryan birthright' is no less racist than the one Griffith could have included as Cameron attacks the cannons. At that point, however, the title is not an interruption to the narrative. Rather, the realisation that white northerners and white southerners share a racial identity that unites them against African Americans *is* the narrative. The coming together of white 'brothers' divided by war is the fundamental structure of the film, whereas in the earlier case, and in innumerable other instances where Griffith cut the racist commentary from Dixon's work, the racism would have been a distraction.

The politics of the film begin to shift after Ben Cameron leaves the hospital and returns home to a devastated Piedmont. In a poignant scene, his younger sister prepares to celebrate his homecoming by draping herself in 'southern ermine' – raw cotton spotted with soot. Our sympathies are with her, but only because of what we do not see – namely, that the economic system of slavery has collapsed because of the war, and the slaves have been freed. Like the rest of the southern aristocracy, her previous comfortable life was based on the economics of harvesting cotton with slaves, and the evils of that system are papered over by the focus on the young girl's needs.

Interspersed with the scenes of homecoming are shots of Stoneman's meeting with Abraham Lincoln in which (referring to the South) Stoneman declares, 'Their leaders must be hanged and their states treated like conquered provinces,' to which Lincoln replies that he 'shall deal with them as though they had never been away'.

A hospital sentry gazes admiringly at Elsie Stoneman; Flora Cameron dresses up in 'southern ermine' – cotton dotted with soot

This exchange sets up the entire second half of the film, since a key part of its political perspective is the idea that, had he lived, Abraham Lincoln would never have imposed Reconstruction.

We move into the scenes of Lincoln's assassination at Ford's Theatre, which is ideal for considering Griffith's style, since the outcome of the scene is preordained. The fact that the audience obviously knows what will happen means that rather than true suspense we have a sense of foreboding, but Griffith masterfully builds the tension by marking the time and showing Lincoln with his wife and entourage entering the theatre by the back stairs to take their place in the private box, setting the scene for the arrival of John Wilkes Booth. Griffith (and Dixon) has fictionalised the scene by adding the two young Stonemans, Elsie and Phil, to the audience, but otherwise the film tries to maintain a strict chronology of the steps that led to the shooting, including a guard leaving his place outside the President's box in order to see the play.

Elsie and Phil Stoneman (foreground) rise to cheer Abraham Lincoln at Ford's Theatre

The film sets up the final assassination sequence with a title card that reads, 'Time, 10:13pm. Act III, Scene 2.' These exact markers serve the larger purpose of demonstrating the film's dedication to historical exactitude, even as the presence of Elsie and Phil Stoneman allows the film to deviate from the official record, especially when Elsie seems to spot John Wilkes Booth just before the assassination. There are repeated point-of-view shots from her perspective, and she seems to mouth to her brother 'Who is that? That man?', before peering at Booth through her opera glasses. The sequence is strange, because at first it is extremely difficult to figure out where Booth is sitting, as all of the close-ups of him are shot in iris. Eventually the iris opens to a wide shot that indicates his place on the balcony, just before he leaves to enter Lincoln's private box. Overall, the spatial relations here are jumpy and not quite 'correct' by classical Hollywood standards, as if Griffith is still working out the details, or perhaps functioning in an earlier mode where a menacing close-up of the villain was more important than clarity of filmed space. There is a second error as Booth sneaks up behind Lincoln: we have seen him draw his gun before opening the door to the private box, and even get a close-up of it glinting in the light, but then he appears to draw it from his jacket again when he is standing directly behind Lincoln a second later.

Booth draws his gun before entering Lincoln's box, then reaches his right hand into his jacket to draw it again once he is inside

Not missing a beat, the film cuts from the assassination of Lincoln to Stoneman hearing the news and a scheming Lydia telling him that he is now the greatest power in America. The reaction in the South is similarly bizarre as the Camerons read the news. The father cries, 'Our best friend is gone. What is to become of us now!' Given that Lincoln had just been the head of the army that had defeated the South, destroyed his property and freed his slaves, it seems unlikely that Master Cameron would refer to him as 'our best friend'. However, the decision to exclude Lincoln from any blame has an important bearing on what happens next, shifting the focus away from the fight over slavery by eliding his role in the institution's demise.

* * *

The second part of *The Birth of a Nation* begins with numerous title cards that reinforce the film's historical veracity. One claims that 'This is an historical presentation of the Civil War and Reconstruction Period, and is not meant to reflect on any race or people of today' – most likely added after the film created controversy. We pivot to the historical argument of the second half, quoting extensively from Woodrow Wilson's *History of the American People*. The first of the two screens of text blames Reconstruction on the carpetbaggers who 'swarmed out of the North, as much the enemies of one race as of the other, to cozen, beguile, and use the negroes'.

As a general rule, the racism of *The Birth of a Nation*, and of Griffith himself, was primarily paternal racism, in which African Americans are seen as children unable to care for themselves, and who thus need the strong and strict guidance of a white overseer.[31] Continuing in this vein, the citation goes on to claim that black office holders in the South 'knew nothing of the uses of authority, except its insolences'. In a move typical of racist thought, the title cards shift immediately from one fear to another. The following card, continuing to quote Wilson, argues that the goal was 'a veritable overthrow of civilization in the South ... in their determination to "put the white

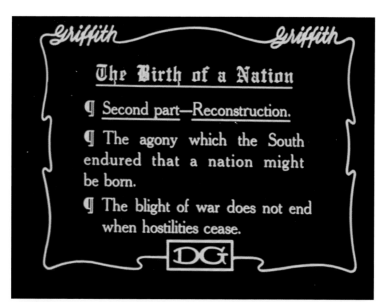

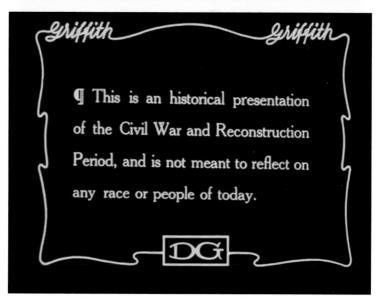

Two title cards from the beginning of the second part of the film

<u>South under the heel of the black South</u>"' (underlining in original). The threat is clear, and in the next card we are informed that 'the white men were roused by a mere instinct of self-preservation'.

It is in the second half that the film's racism becomes much more overt, and does so in a way that tells us a great deal about mainstream beliefs in 1915. In an early scene in which the 'uncrowned king' Austin Stoneman greets guests in his office, he tells the mulatto Silas Lynch, 'Don't scrape to me. You are the equal of any man here.' To a modern audience, it is possible to read this statement with the inverse of its actual meaning. Stoneman is repudiating discrimination, something we now commend. Given the rhetorical structure of the film though, it is clearly intended to further mark Stoneman as a villain. There is also a revealing exchange later when Lynch arrives in Piedmont and Ben Cameron declines to shake his hand, which is presented as a demonstration of high-minded principle. Cameron also refuses to share the sidewalk

'Don't scrape to me': a belief in equality played as villainy

with blacks, something he would not have been accustomed to doing before the war.

There have been many defences of *The Birth of a Nation*'s racism over the past century, and the strongest of them have underscored the context of the film's production – that the historical records of the time endorsed this view of Reconstruction, and that it was intended to be a historical film, as its titles claimed, rather than a portrait of the 'present day' of 1915.[32] But there is no way to reconcile that view with these incidents, where the film cannot hide behind 'historical' justifications for its perspectives on race. In exchanges like the two above, the mere idea of racial equality is presented as despicable, with racism seen as the highest virtue. To make it clear in Stoneman's elevation of Lynch, the next title declares that 'The great Radical delivers his edict that the blacks shall be raised to full equality with the whites.' This and Cameron's refusal to share the sidewalk or shake hands are supposed to horrify us, not because someone would have proposed racial equality in 1865, but that such an idea could be proposed *at any time and place*. To argue otherwise is to ignore the film's entire narrative structure and mode of address.

The repercussions of political equality are spelled out in the next scene in Stoneman's apartment, as he sends Lynch south to 'aid the carpetbaggers in organising and wielding the power of the negro vote'. When Elsie appears, innocently arranging flowers, Lynch gives her a longing look. Unlike the earlier scene in the hospital where the sentry watched Elsie arrive and leave, this episode is not intended to be funny or charming. *The Birth of a Nation* mirrors the racist imagination's view of African Americans as alternately childishly innocent or deviously evil depending on which stereotype serves the necessary purpose.

As the film's version of Reconstruction takes hold across the South, black field workers are induced to throw down their tools and start dancing, and we are told that 'The charity of a generous North [was] misused to delude the ignorant.' While there is not space here to offer a point-by-point rebuttal of Dixon and Griffith's version of the Reconstruction, it is worth noting – in broad outlines where possible – the most egregious errors, especially since we have historical accounts of the end of slavery written from a slave perspective. The most famous of these is perhaps that of Booker T. Washington, the educator who was born a slave in Virginia and went on to found the Tuskegee Institute. Washington was hardly a radical, even by late-nineteenth and early twentieth-century standards, and continually preached a doctrine of uplift through education and the development of trades by African Americans. He describes the announcement of freedom on his plantation like this:

For some minutes there was great rejoicing, and thanksgiving, and wild scenes of ecstasy. But there was no feeling of bitterness. In fact, there was pity among the slaves for our former owners. The wild rejoicing on the part of the emancipated coloured people lasted but for a brief period, for I noticed that by the time they returned to their cabins there was a change in their feelings. The great responsibility of being free, of having charge of themselves, of having to think and plan for themselves and their children, seemed to take possession of them. It was very much like suddenly turning a youth of ten or twelve years out into the world to provide for himself. In a few hours the great questions with which the Anglo-Saxon race had been grappling for

Elsie catches Silas Lynch looking at her; the two are maintained in separate shots

centuries had been thrown upon these people to be solved. These were the questions of a home, a living, the rearing of children, education, citizenship, and the establishment and support of churches. Was it any wonder that within a few hours the wild rejoicing ceased and a feeling of deep gloom seemed to pervade the slave quarters? To some it seemed that, now that they were in actual possession of it, freedom was a more serious thing than they had expected to find it. Some of the slaves were seventy or eighty years old; their best days were gone. They had no strength with which to earn a living in a strange place and among strange people, even if they had been sure where to find a new place of abode. To this class the problem seemed especially hard. Besides, deep down in their hearts there was a strange and peculiar attachment to 'old Marster' and 'old Missus', and to their children, which they found it hard to think of breaking off. With these they had spent in some cases nearly a half-century, and it was no light thing to think of parting. Gradually, one by one, stealthily at first, the older slaves began to wander from the slave quarters back to the 'big house' to have a whispered conversation with their former owners as to the future.[33]

Washington goes on to write that, although his own family eventually moved away to West Virginia, many of the older slaves simply stayed where they were and became employees for meagre wages. We tend to think of the end of slavery in broad historical terms, but it is helpful to see it as a rupture, when slaves would have had to confront a completely new life and a new world, but with almost no resources – no money, no education and, in many cases, no experience of living anywhere outside of their own plantation.

Instead of the remarkably peaceful transitions that Washington describes, we might imagine an alternative historical record in which freed slaves saw the end of the Civil War as a chance to avenge their own enslavement and maltreatment, and routinely attacked their former masters. From our present-day perspective, that they did not do so seems like admirable restraint. Washington and other correspondents of the period make it clear that slaves internalised the system of slavery enough to develop strong attachments to their masters and to the white families who were dependent on their labour; however, while Washington details stories of slave loyalty at length, he is emphatic that 'From some things that I have said one may get the idea that some of the slaves did not want freedom. This is not true. I have never seen one who did not want to be free, or one who would return to slavery.'[34]

This is the error that Griffith and many others made – mistaking the closeness and loyalty that slavery sometimes engendered for an endorsement of slavery itself, and failing to see the flaws in a system in which black people's role is to serve and protect. Griffith was unabashedly nostalgic for this era in at least this sense, and two of his earlier films, *His Trust* and *His Trust Fulfilled* (both 1911), tell the story of a loyal slave who keeps the family's belongings safe while they are away. The narrative is nearly identical to some of the stories recounted by Washington elsewhere in his memoir, but in Washington's case they are arguments for the character of black people despite an oppressive system, not a justification for that system. Defending *The Birth of a Nation*, Griffith sometimes argued that the film was not racist, because it showed the bad along with the good. By this he meant the pair of Cameron slaves who display fierce loyalty to their former masters and seem to share their white counterparts' disgust for the idea of black equality.

In the second half of *The Birth of a Nation*, the filmic innovations become harder to see through the politics, but they are of course still there. One example occurs when Elsie Stoneman, played by Lillian Gish, meets young Flora Cameron for the first time. As Flora hugs and embraces her enthusiastically, Gish looks alternately terrified, then confused, then relieved, as she figures out who this girl is. Throughout her career, Gish became expert at portraying shifts in emotional state using only her facial expressions, and was eventually able to demonstrate extremely subtle shifts in character mood and emotion, and do it quickly and naturally. By the end of the silent era, she had mastered silent film acting like few others, as her performances in films like *The Scarlet Letter* (1926)

ably demonstrate. In her autobiography, Gish credits this ability in part to Griffith:

'Expression without distortion,' he always said. He meant, 'Frown without frowning.' Show disapproval without unsightly wrinkles … I learned from him to use my body and face quite impersonally to create effects, much as a painter uses paint on canvas. Later on, when I worked with other directors, I would hang a mirror at the side of the camera, so that in closeup I could see what effect I was producing.[35]

After Ben Cameron has refused to shake Silas Lynch's hand (which the title attributes to 'the black's condescension'), there is a slightly unusual use of cross-cutting, as we move back and forth between Ben and Elsie on the porch and Stoneman and Lynch inside the house. With no real tension building here, and not much happening in either scene that calls for contrast, the cross-cutting

Elsie meets Flora for the first time

serves only to provide a sense of pace and movement. Griffith had been an early adopter of cross-cutting and used it to great effect many times, usually to create dramatic climaxes. This small example in the house demonstrates a much more assured and casual mastery of editing.

Electoral politics briefly move into the foreground as Stoneman and Lynch and their allies enjoy a political victory, and Ben Cameron recounts to his friends a series of 'outrages' that have occurred, including white people being put on trial 'before a negro magistrate and the verdict rendered against the whites by the negro jury'. White citizens are shown being roughed up by soldiers, while the 'faithful family servant' is punished for not voting with the carpetbaggers. As he tells the story, the framing seems strangely off centre, since Ben and the other men occupy the bottom of the image, with the staircase filling the screen behind them. What seems like a cinematographic miscue is soon revealed to be careful

Ben Cameron's refusal to shake hands with a black man (who is the friend of his guests) is presented as high-minded principle

planning, however, as Ben rises from his seat to fill the frame, fist curled in outrage, before an iris frames him looking passionately to the heavens.

In her article 'History as Pretext', Mimi White considers the use of footnotes in the sequence of the South Carolina legislature, titled 'The riot in the Master's Hall.' The card reads, in part, 'An historical facsimile of the State House of Representatives of South Carolina as it was in 1870. After photograph by "The Columbia State".' It is here that historical *mise en scène* is most literally used to make up for a fictionalised narrative, since, as White points out, the footnote refers to a *photograph* of the South Carolina statehouse, not to any of the events we are about to see. The scene opens with an image of the empty statehouse (the information referred to in the footnote), before a dissolve (one of only a couple in the film) to a shot of black legislators sitting with their feet on desks, eating and generally misbehaving. The purpose of the dissolve is to blur the line between

Cameron recounts the outrages that have occurred in the name of equality

what can be verified and what is made up, and to provide historical cover for the latter.[36]

In the legislature scene, we see black representatives eyeing white women in the balcony and then immediately voting to allow the intermarriage of blacks and whites, again reinforcing the notion that the pursuit of white women by black men was a common phenomenon, when in fact the power differentials of the period meant that it was much more frequently the other way around.[37] The scenes of legislators jubilantly celebrating what is inferred to be open season on white women is not enough, however – the politically useful fear must be made more explicit, perhaps since in reality it would have been so far from common experience. The next title card reads, 'Later. The grim reaping begins,' and here there is a substantial difference between versions of the film. In copies that seem to be based on the 1915 prints of the film (which have a title card that refers viewers to the printed programme, rather than the rolling

The photograph of the empty South Carolina legislature, referenced with a footnote, dissolves into this image of the chamber full of representatives, deliberately blurring the line between history and fiction

credits which appeared later), the sequence of scenes is about three and a half minutes long. In the first part, Elsie and Flora run off to a park and sit talking and hugging, unaware that they are being watched by Gus, who the titles tell us is 'a product of the vicious doctrines spread by the carpetbaggers'. In the second section, Flora and Elsie meet Silas Lynch after leaving the park, and Flora is horrified when Elsie shakes his hand. Ben Cameron appears and directs disapproving looks at Lynch, who just grins. In the last part, Flora is on her front porch and Gus comes to stare at her. Ben arrives home and tells Gus to leave, starting a dispute that draws the attention of Silas Lynch, who reprimands Ben and tells Gus to let him know if he has this problem again.

In most copies of the film with rolling credits, which are likely to date from the later 1910s or 20s, the first part of this sequence is significantly shorter, the second part is intact and the third part has been excised completely, so that the entire sequence now lasts about a minute and a half – two whole minutes are missing. It seems unlikely that any of this would have been censored, since there is much worse to come between Gus and Flora, and many of the cuts are barely noticeable. More probably, this is the hand of Griffith changing his film simply to make it work better. The recut version minimises what seem to be errors in the earlier version.

In the first part of the sequence in the park, the cuts do not change the fundamental construction of the scene. Flora and Elsie are confiding and laughing like sisters, and Gus is watching them. The missing shots are mostly repetitive, and some of the existing ones have been trimmed so that, for example, Gus is already in place at the beginning of the sequence rather than wandering in. The net effect is a subtle change in the geography of the scene, since Flora and Elsie now seem to be sitting directly behind the spot where we first see Gus (near a tree and a fence that we have seen in an earlier shot of Ben Cameron), and which appears to be right next to the Cameron house. In the longer version, the park is clearly further away from the house. The only substantive change is the loss of a close-up of Gus, which

adds to his menace and would more clearly signal to the audience what is to come. Any one of these cuts could just be a break in the film or a damaged frame or a censor's hand, but in sum they indicate a deliberate set of choices, almost undoubtedly Griffith's revisions.

More complicated but still likely to be Griffith's hand are the drastic changes in the third part of the sequence, when Gus gets into an argument with Ben Cameron at the Camerons' front gate. The problem with this scene in both versions is that we see Flora and Elsie meet Silas Lynch on a town street, and they are standing on a porch at what could be mistaken for the Camerons' house, although it clearly is not (there is no fence, the pillars are plain and there are more people in the background). After Elsie greets Lynch, and Flora leaves in apparent disgust, we see Flora again a few shots later on the porch of her own house. The confusion is that because her porch is similar enough to the one she was standing near a minute before, it looks like she has reappeared in the same space as Lynch and Ben Cameron, who are apparently supposed to be somewhere else in town. The illusion that they are standing near each other is aided by what appears to be a shot/reverse-shot sequence with an eyeline match, in which Lynch looks off to the right and Flora looks to the left. To anyone not paying very close attention, they appear to be clearly looking at each other from a few feet away, even though this is impossible. In the longer

Flora Cameron, on her own front porch, appears to make eye contact with Lynch, who is somewhere else in town; Lynch appears to return the stare

version, Gus reappears at Flora's gate and, unlike Lynch, he really is staring at her, but the transition is very confusing.

Without the scene of Gus at the gate, the mismatched spaces are less obvious. Lynch and Flora still have their impossible shot/reverse shot with an eyeline match, but because the scene is over quickly we are less likely to register that Flora is on her own porch, even when Elsie joins her there a shot later. That Griffith was indeed fixing an error is supported by the fact that it is not just whole shots that are missing. In the shorter version, once Elsie has left the scene, we cut away from Flora before she enters the house. Having her walk through the door makes it clear that this is her home, but if the scene simply ends without the entrance, it is possible to not notice where she is standing, and we move on.

We can never know for sure the path that our various copies of *The Birth of a Nation* have taken, and whose hands have been on them, but we have many accounts of Griffith recutting his film continually after its release, and censor records to support some of the more common variations (such as the earlier scene of Austin Stoneman touching his maid's bare shoulder). In cases like this, where the cuts are trims of multiple shots, we can assume that they are artistic in nature rather than censorious or accidental. The net effect of the changes in this scene is to push us towards the action of the film more quickly and give away less of what is to come.

What is to come, of course, is the rise of the Ku Klux Klan, and the re-enactment of its 'inspiration' is particularly horrifying, since it involves Cameron watching white children scare black children with a white sheet. To modern eyes, the contrast between what the Klan represents to us and Cameron's happy smile as he realises what he must do is a particularly chilling moment in the film. The title card that follows is one of the few to offer any critique of the Klan, however mild. It calls the KKK, 'the organization that saved the South from the anarchy of black rule, but not without the shedding of more blood than at Gettysburg, according to Judge Tourgee of the carpet-baggers'. While its attribution to a carpetbagger undermines

the critique, and it is an exaggeration, it is remarkable that it is
there at all. There is certainly no hint that the Klan is anything but
honourable in the next few scenes, in which the group's riders
'terrorize a negro disturber and barn burner', although the film
maintains their heroic underdog position by showing Lynch and his
supporters scoring 'first blood' and shooting several Klansmen from
a hidden position. Soon enough, Stoneman is mouthing the words
that Woodrow Wilson's book had created for him: 'We will crush
the white south under the heel of the black south.'[38] When Elsie
arrives and is told that her lover 'belongs to this murderous band
of outlaws', the title is, in some versions, oddly misplaced, appearing
as she walks into the room rather than a few seconds later when
Stoneman actually speaks the words. In other versions, the title is
placed 'correctly', in line with Griffith's practice. It seems like
another fix, except that the copies with the misplaced title appear
to be later versions, and there is no visible seam in the shot of Elsie
and Stoneman speaking to suggest the title has been moved. This is
simply another version mystery, as there is no straightforward
explanation for the differences.

In the scenes that follow, some of the differences between
versions are easier to comprehend. In the extended sequence in which
Gus chases Flora through the woods and up to the top of a hill,
several shots of him are missing in many versions, and this scene is
frequently referenced in censorship papers. The most common
omissions are two medium shots of Gus gesturing at Flora from only
a few feet away at the top of the hill. In one, his words and actions
are ambiguous, and when he waves his arms at her it is not clear if he
is trying to stop her from jumping or daring her to do so. In any
event, the scene was often one censors had trouble with because of
the implied attempt at rape. Although Gus announces to Flora that
he wants to get married, the clear indication is that he is about to
rape her, which is underscored by the title: 'For her who had learned
the stern lesson of honor we should not grieve that she found sweeter
the <u>opal gates of death</u>' (underlining in original).

Even by the standards of traditional femininity in play at the time, this scene is extremely conservative in terms of gender. While we have noted how the fear of black men attacking white women was used as an excuse to control both groups, this title makes explicit that, had she chosen to live, the rape would have been, in some ways, her fault. The 'stern lesson of honor' is that honour is more valuable than life, and that it is preferable to die rather than to be raped. Thus, the safeguarding of honour is a strong incentive for women to stay in the house. Not only are there risks if they leave, but anything that happens to them endangers their purity, which is their most valuable asset. This fetishisation of purity is taken to a more bizarre extreme in a later Klan ceremony, where Ben dips a flag in what is apparently Flora's blood, then uses it to quench the flames of a burning cross, calling it 'the sweetest blood that ever stained the sands of Time!' He also refers to the cross as 'the fiery cross of old Scotland's hills', the only time the film makes explicit the Klan's

Gus approaches the little sister on the mountain top

frequent use of a mythical version of Scotland to establish its history and foundations.[39]

In between Flora's death and the ceremony, there is an action sequence of Gus's arrest and 'fair trial'. The variations in this scene are about continuity and clarity, but may be caused in part by damage to one of the prints. As Ben enlists townsmen in the hunt for Gus, two young men in the carriage shop decide to join the search and one, in a white shirt, sets off to the gin mill where he suspects (correctly) that Gus is hiding. His friend, wearing a darker shirt, goes off in another direction. White shirt finds Gus in the gin mill and in an extended sequence fights off all of its patrons, only to be shot by the bartender as he leaves and then be finished off by Gus. Dark shirt witnesses all this and sets off after Gus. It is this same young man who shoots Gus off his horse a minute later. In many versions of the film, this is not very clear, since some of the shots of the two young men together are truncated or cut completely, and they look similar other than their clothes. In some versions, the dark-shirted man raises his gun to shoot Gus, and we see Gus fall off his horse, but the smoke from his shot has been cut, presumably because it was considered too violent.

Some other scenes were cut and are now lost, most famously a sequence from the end of the film that showed 'Lincoln's solution' of repatriating blacks to Africa. A review in the trade journal *Motion Picture World* on 13 March 1915 mentions this and several other segments or titles that do not survive, including a segment early in the film claiming that 'when slave trading was no longer profitable to the North the "traders of the seventeenth century became the abolitionists of the nineteenth century"' and a title that describes the Klan as riding to punish 'wicked Africans'.[40]

Some scenes that were cut do survive, however, including one in which Margaret Cameron and her mother are confronted at their front gate by a well-dressed African-American woman. The scene, which survives on a reel of outtakes preserved at the Library of Congress, would have added some complexity to the film, since the

black people who interact with the Camerons are almost exclusively male, imparting a sense of menace and foreboding in line with the film's claims about the threat of black masculinity. In the existing version, the woman from the outtake does appear in the film after Master Cameron is arrested and 'paraded before his former slaves' in a clear inversion of what is supposed to be the natural order. Played by an African-American woman rather than a white actor in blackface, she laughs and taunts him before he is led away in chains. Most sources identify this actress as Madame Sul-Te-Wan (born Nellie Conley in 1873), who appeared in dozens of films over the next forty years, although generally limited to the stereotypical roles available to African-American actors.[41]

The jeers of the former slaves, generally portrayed by African-American extras, are soon contrasted by the actions of the two 'faithful souls' who save Master Cameron. They 'pretend to join the mockers'. Mingling with the soldiers, the male servant (he is never named) taunts Master Cameron by saying 'Is I yo' equal cap'n – jes

An outtake from the film, not included in any surviving versions, in which a well-dressed African-American woman confronts Margaret Cameron and her mother outside their house

like any white man?' This is supposed to be a joke – a servant saying something ridiculous that only a radical would believe, and performed by a white actor in blackface.[42] It is a complicated episode, because freeing Master Cameron is supposed to be the highest achievement of the two servants, and the film includes the comic line as an example of the servant's skill at pretending to be what he is not. Thus, we are supposed to admire him for being intelligent and witty enough to make the remark, while simultaneously laughing at the idea that he could ever be equal to a white man. In this case, the man is putting his duplicitousness to good use, but it is very much on display. Thus, although Griffith held up these 'faithful souls' as examples of 'good' black characters, they are not simply caricatures of simple and reliable servants. Even these noble characters, we are reminded, are capable of being sly and underhanded. The female servant, named Mammy in the credits, is equally able to fool the soldiers, but also uses her ample size to pin them to the ground, an action intended to be comically grotesque. All of this is on top of the fact that the two servants are fighting to save their master, who has been arrested for being a member of the Klan, implying either that they support the Klan or that it is incomprehensible to them.

One of the soldiers is slain by Phil Stoneman, and this sets in motion the climax of the film, as some of the Stonemans and Camerons take refuge in a small cabin with two former Union soldiers, so that 'The former enemies of North and South are united again in common defence of their Aryan birthright.' This is the most notorious title in the film, and for good reason, because it makes explicit what has until now been forcefully implied – that this is not a story about the mismanagement of the Reconstruction, but about the reconciliations that are necessary among the white brotherhood in the face of a black menace. The word 'Aryan' has an even more negative punch for present-day viewers because of its use by Nazis, but its meaning was clear in 1915. That word overshadows everything else in the sentence, but it is worth considering the notion

that they are 'united again', since this ties back to the claim in the very first title of the movie that it was the bringing of 'the African' to the New World that had 'planted the first seed of disunion'. Slavery is, in Dixon's construction much more than Griffith's, an interruption in the development of white brotherhood in the United States, one that peaks with the Civil War and Reconstruction, and can now be overcome with a recognition of that Aryan birthright. This notion, of a birthright to the United States, plays into several fundamental ideas in American culture of the period. Among them is the concept of 'unalienable Rights' found in the Declaration of Independence and extended over the centuries. Originally, of course, the writers of the Declaration and the US Constitution had no sense that any of the rights they were discussing applied to black people, or even fully to women. Such notions were certainly not settled propositions in 1915, when black men could vote (at least in the North) but women could not.

Mammy uses her size to overcome an occupying soldier

The idea of a birthright also resonates with the American notion of Manifest Destiny – that the United States was the natural ruler of all of North America, with no place for native peoples or, for that matter, Canadians. For North America to be a place to which Aryans have a birthright, it has to be clear that the native people who lived there had no such rights, and there would have been no sense of 'native rights' in 1915. Even the Declaration of Independence, a high-minded document filled with references to self-evident truths and the consent of the governed, refers to native peoples as 'the merciless Indian savages'. In the 1910s and 20s, at the peak of a nativist fervour in the United States, with calls for the restriction of immigration and the acceptability of eugenics, the notion of an 'Aryan birthright' would have seemed simple and obvious to a majority of white Americans. By the sound-era re-release of *The Birth of a Nation* in 1930, the mood had shifted enough that the title card was rewritten to complain only of 'the carpetbaggers' mad folly'. As part of the redesign of *The Birth of a Nation* as a simpler action and adventure story, there was less need to wrap it up in political claims.

The rewritten 1930 title about the 'carpetbaggers' mad folly' does not actually make much difference in historical terms. It is another kind of historical lie, and seems expressly designed to be less offensive and more neutral, but it does not in fact change the argument of the film – that Reconstruction is the reason why these white people have found themselves under attack by black soldiers. Silas Lynch's proposal of marriage to Elsie is in the same category. It is one of the few titles rewritten in 1930 to be more inflammatory – the neutral words 'Lynch's proposal of marriage' become 'The black's mad proposal of marriage.' A later title about building 'a Black Empire' with Elsie as its queen becomes simply 'an empire'. Either way, Elsie's reaction is to threaten him with 'a horsewhipping for his insolence' for even suggesting such a thing, and to react with horror as his seriousness becomes clear. It is here that Lynch becomes truly freakish – the lighting, his movements and Elsie's

reaction all suggest that rather than a human being, he is a monster created with human parts.

Shots of assembling Klansmen begin to be intercut with the scenes of Elsie and Lynch. There is no justification for this assembly yet – the Klansmen are unaware of Elsie's predicament and of the people in the cabin. Significant differences between the order of shots begin to emerge in various prints at this point. Some have a title that reads 'Summoning the Klans', as a pair of fast-moving riders gallop through the woods and past farms sounding a call, so that the group becomes larger and larger. Other prints retain some shots of these two riders, but the 'Summoning' title is inserted later, long after most of the Klansmen have assembled. There are other revealing differences: the most complete prints have at least one slow dissolve between the shots of a pair of riders rushing to call the others, reinforcing the aesthetic effect of the carefully composed sequence; and the series of shots in which Austin Stoneman arrives back in

In this shot from an outtake reel preserved at the Library of Congress, Lillian Gish and George Siegmann rehearse the scene in which Silas Lynch proposes to Elsie Stoneman. Note that this set becomes the foyer of Austin Stoneman's office in the film (see p. 30)

Piedmont varies considerably in its placement, apparently reflecting
once again Griffith's changing tastes and aesthetic preferences after
the film was released.

The revelation in which Austin Stoneman learns of Lynch's
plans to marry his daughter provides both Stoneman's comeuppance
– this is what you get for supporting equality – and a further
demonstration of his hypocrisy, since he has just nodded supportively
when Lynch declares that he wants to marry a white woman.
The categories of race become even more complicated a few seconds
later, when Elsie goes to the window and is spotted by 'White Spies
Disguised' – two Klansmen on horseback wearing blackface. It is a
curious scene, since – like Lynch and Mammy, and nearly all of the
other black and mixed-race characters – these are white actors in
blackface. Nevertheless, we are supposed to know the difference
between Lynch and these white men disguised in makeup. In one
sense, the film undoes everything it has just spent hours building up

'White spies disguised'

by calling attention to the blackface and the supposed ease with which it provides a disguise. At the same time, it is claiming that blackface is an effective disguise within the 'real' world of the film – that two white men can move among a crowd of black people unnoticed simply by painting their faces. It thus normalises the use of blackface by inferring that there is no difference between makeup and an actual black face. We already know, however, from the rest of the film, that racial differences are not skin deep at all, but reflections of intrinsic capability and character.

There is no way to reconcile this scene with the ideology of the rest of the film, because it reveals one of the limitations of the screen as a medium. In a novel, one can simply describe a person as disguised without having to confront the construction of the rest of the black characters. On film (or on stage), one needs black bodies to play the roles, but if 'on careful weighing of every detail concerned, the decision was to have no black blood among the principals'[43] (as Griffith chose to do when casting *Birth of a Nation*), then the contradictions of blackface cannot be avoided. The interplay of two deeply entrenched theatrical traditions, however, meant that audiences at the time would probably not have been troubled by the contradictions. The first, of course, is the overwhelming and complicated history of blackface itself, used for nearly a century in a variety of formats and media, sometimes to mock African Americans and sometimes adopted by African-American performers themselves.[44] Blackface was therefore completely unremarkable to audiences in 1915. In addition, there is the much broader theatrical tradition of disguised characters who are obvious to the audience in the theatre but who are able to fool the other characters in the play. Shakespeare is full of such examples, and audiences have been trained to play along. The development of special effects and film makeup in the past century has meant that audiences expect higher and higher standards of verisimilitude when it comes to actors in disguise, but there is always some knowledge of the person underneath the mask that must be set aside. Despite these traditions, this moment in *The Birth of a Nation* is a complicated one.

The white spies are disguising themselves just at the moment the villains are being revealed. Lynch has already locked Elsie in, and her screams for help are heard by her father, who now begins to struggle with Lynch. The complexity of Griffith's editing becomes evident here – we have cuts within the numerous rooms of Lynch's house, a quick shot of black soldiers finding the broken cart abandoned by the Stonemans and Camerons, and then we are in the cabin as the soldiers catch up with them. To give us a sense of the time that has elapsed between the discovery of the cart and the arrival of the soldiers, we see multiple shots of the people in the cabin, including a quite beautiful irised close-up of a pensive Margaret Cameron. The effect is to provide a short pause before the action and the gunshots resume, and to demonstrate the subtlety of Griffith's skill, since he is aware that what comes after will seem faster and more exciting after a brief respite. The shots that follow cut from place to place and set the stage for the final confrontation. The cabin dwellers are poised to fight, Klansmen are on the move, and Elsie is now bound and gagged with a fist poised at her head. We are told that this is happening 'While helpless whites looked on', and we see families posed in interior scenes, reading the bible and looking heavenwards. There are about half a dozen such scenes, each contrasted with images of black rioters in the streets.

In Joseph Carl Breil's score, we hear repeated fast motifs that fail to resolve, creating a strong sense of anticipation.[45] As the Klansmen arrive in Piedmont to break up the riots and rescue Elsie, the music shifts to a version of the instantly recognisable 'Ride of the Valkyries' theme from Wagner's *Die Walküre*, which will be repeated throughout the climax of the film. *The Birth of a Nation* was one of the first films to have a set score, rather than being accompanied by whatever the musician in the theatre decided to play, which was the case for the majority of silent cinema. Breil toured with the film in some cities, conducting the orchestra himself, and the score is a mix

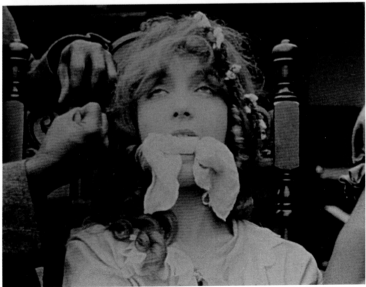

Margaret Cameron in the little cabin; Elsie is tied up in preparation for her forced marriage to Lynch

of original and canonical works. The use of Wagner here is interesting for a number of reasons. This particular piece has been used in film many times since, most famously for the napalm bombing scene in Francis Ford Coppola's *Apocalypse Now*. Wagner himself was a virulent anti-Semite whose music was very popular with the Nazis and who has suffered for that association ever since. It was not, for example, performed publicly in Israel until 2001 (and even then not without controversy), with more recent performances having been cancelled after protests.[46] Given this history, it is especially disconcerting that the music also appears in a film like *The Birth of a Nation* to accompany the ride of the Ku Klux Klan.

The climax of *The Birth of a Nation* offers two rescues in one, befitting a film of this length and scope. Elsie must be rescued from the clutches of Silas Lynch, and then the people in the cabin must be saved. The first clashes take place in the streets of Piedmont, and there are some intense battle scenes with casualties on both sides.

The Klan rides to the rescue

After Elsie and her father are rescued, the music switches away from
Wagner for a few minutes before resuming the Valkyries theme once
again. In these sequences, Griffith demonstrates the sure mastery of
editing techniques he had developed in his years of making one-
and two-reel films. Here the drama is further intensified by what
happens in the cabin as the soldiers begin to break down the doors.
Master Cameron holds a pistol over the head of his daughter
Margaret, apparently ready to smash her skull rather than let her fall
into the hands of the black soldiers. One of the white Union veterans
holds a door with one hand and a rifle in the other, ready to bring the
butt of it down on the head of the youngest daughter should the door
give way. Everything is at stake – not only death but a loss of honour
the characters fear much more. We cut from close-ups of the terrified
child to gleeful soldiers smashing down the door, and to Margaret
Cameron, hair held back by her father, calmly accepting her fate.
At the last second, of course, the Klansmen arrive and save the day.

Dr Cameron prepares to smash his daughter's skull with the butt of a revolver rather
than let her fall into the hands of the renegade soldiers

In the shorter version of *The Birth of a Nation* released in 1930, there is no denouement. After the rescue, we see the 'Parade of the liberators' (earlier 'Parade of the Klansmen'), and then the movie is over. The effect is to strip much of the social and political context out of the film, whereas the original version finishes by raising the stakes even further. In the original, after some shots of the other white families from the town breathing sighs of relief, we flash forward to 'The Next Election', where intimidated African Americans are forced back into their homes by Klansmen on horseback, a scene that makes it clear that continuing efforts to disenfranchise black citizens, commonplace in 1915, are necessary for the survival of the country. In the next future scene, 'At the sea's edge, a double honeymoon', a matte shot of Margaret Cameron and Phil Stoneman looking out over an ocean is followed by one of Elsie Stoneman and Ben Cameron sitting on a cliff.

It would be hard to imagine a finale more ambitious in scope – a final scene that asks, 'Dare we dream of a golden day when the bestial War shall rule no more. But instead – the gentle Prince in the Hall of Brotherly Love in the City of Peace.' The devil sits upon a horse and taunts the damned, who include women with small children, next to a pile of corpses wearing the costumes of various eras. A larger-than-life apparition of Jesus moves his hand calmly over a scene of a joyous heaven, and the people briefly fade out to leave only Jesus himself. Everyone in both heaven and hell is white.

When heaven reappears, the image of Jesus has been replaced in the centre of the frame by an image of a shining city on a hill. In the final shot of the film, this same city is combined in a double exposure with the image of Ben and Elsie overlooking the sea, so that the personal future they are envisaging becomes an idealised social future for their white descendants and for the United States of America. To make this clear, the final title calls for 'Liberty and union, one and inseparable, now and forever!' (underlining in original), as Breil's score finishes with 'The Star Spangled Banner', a motif deeply disturbing to contemporary Americans, who have

At 'the next election', the KKK prevents African Americans from voting; a honeymoon at the sea's edge

The film's vision of hell; Jesus presides over an all-white heaven

much more positive associations with their national anthem. At the time, however, there would have been no contradiction, and the film was merely completing the task promised in its title – to connect the pain and division of the Civil War to a broader national identity in the present day of 1915, and to inspire audiences with the promise of a purer, whiter, future.

* * *

Defenders of Griffith often argue that he was a southerner raised in a family with Confederate connections, and thus a product of his time. This is a crucial point, not simply to give Griffith an 'excuse' (even though that is what we are doing in part) but to have a better sense of how racist ideologies could function. Although Griffith never apologised for *The Birth of a Nation*, and indeed saw himself as a persecuted victim of intolerance, there is little evidence that he actually supported the radically racist politics of Thomas Dixon,

The political and the personal are linked as Ben Cameron and Elsie Stoneman look forward to the future

in which black people pose an irredeemable threat. His racism, as we have noted, was generally the paternal type. In this view, Reconstruction was a terrible mistake, because it attempted to give the rights and responsibilities of citizenship to those who were not capable of exercising them. Having grown up with family stories of the evils of Reconstruction and the glory of the Confederacy, and with an academic historical consensus to back up that view, Griffith was shocked that anyone could disagree with him or attack him, especially when he regarded *The Birth of a Nation* as a *historical* story, even adding a disclaimer to that effect before the second half of the film. If anything, the sins that black people were accused of in the film were, to Griffith, evidence of how far African Americans had come in only fifty years. As controversy mounted, some versions of the film even played with what became known as the 'Hampton epilogue': documentary footage of African-American students at the Hampton Institute learning trades and developing work skills. The supposed depravities of the Reconstruction era were thus contrasted with the successes of the present in 1915.[47]

D. W. Griffith was not primarily motivated by hatred of African Americans in the way that Thomas Dixon genuinely appears to have been. To Griffith, this was first and foremost a compelling and exciting tale; had he found another story he could have told in a similar manner, he might have chosen that instead. From all evidence, he was motivated by narrative and the possibilities of film rather than by animosity. Yet, despite that, he is the director of perhaps the most viciously racist film ever to see wide release, a film that colours his legacy and has cost him some of his credit in the pantheon of cinema directors. To choose just the most obvious example, the Directors Guild of America first awarded the D. W. Griffith Lifetime Achievement Award in 1953, but in 1999, they dropped Griffith's name from the title. Their website now lists all past winners as recipients of the DGA Lifetime Achievement Award, regardless of which year it was awarded. This move was controversial at the time, given Griffith's nearly singular contribution to American film-making, and it is a good example of the challenge involved in weighing his work against the content of this film, a balance that has surely shifted over time to a greater sensitivity regarding the history and legacy of racism. It is also hard to imagine that the United States Postal Service would put Griffith on a stamp in the twenty-first century, as they did in 1975.

That Griffith saw his film as a work of history also demonstrates something important about the way we look at historical fiction films. Among film scholars, the default theory has long been a postmodern one, in which notions of truth are de-emphasised in favour of seeing history as contextual, contested and constructed. This position has several long and complicated roots, which cannot be fully recounted here, but it is in line with a broader acceptance of postmodernism in the humanities, and a general scepticism about the truth claims of both history and science. Scholars such as Hayden White, who argues that the narrative conventions of written history have a much greater effect on our historical imagination than we like to admit, have been influential.[48] The postmodern position has also been reinforced by a defensive reaction to the complaints of academic historians, who have, not surprisingly, tended to evaluate historical dramas in relation to their fidelity to written accounts. Film scholars are often more interested in films as works of art and see them as historical documents of their time of production. We are not, as a general rule, interested in what a particular film says about the past other than as a document of the times or the people who made it. The actual historical veracity of a historical film is often seen as being of minor relevance. Where film scholars have been interested in debates about historical accuracy, they have tended to be robust defenders of the right of film-makers to make their art unencumbered by close attention to historical facts, and then, when pushed, have fallen back to the notion that historical facts are constructed anyway. This last position may not be held particularly strongly, given that when film scholars write or read film history, they maintain a traditional modernist emphasis on researched facts that can be documented with written records. Thus, in theory, there is a deep epistemological rift between film scholars and academic historians on the nature of historical fact. In practice, they work in almost identical modes.[49]

The tendency of film scholars to be postmodernists in theory makes a lot of disciplinary sense. In almost all cases, the actual historical veracity of a historical fiction film is outside of the scope of what film scholars do. Given the relatively short history of film studies, and the fact that film itself has only recently been considered an art form at all, it has made sense for scholars to avoid critical positions that make film dependent on written forms. Film scholars seldom compare literary adaptations with their written sources (most of the publications in this area come from literary studies itself), and when comparisons are made, it is never with the idea that the written text is the 'real' one and that adaptations can be judged only by their fidelity to the original. Such an approach would establish film as a secondary form, an idea sharply at odds with the idea of cinema as an art in its own right. By the same token, film scholars tend to downplay or excuse historical errors as unimportant or irrelevant.

No film challenges this perspective as deeply as *The Birth of a Nation*. It is impossible to assess the film in the present day without making the fact that it is *not true* central to one's approach. One cannot leave its distortions aside, or argue that it is an equally valid version of history, or, most importantly, claim that its correspondence to actual history is irrelevant. This is not just a moral question, but an intellectual one – to claim in the present day that *The Birth of a Nation*'s relationship to the history of the Reconstruction is irrelevant is to miss the point completely.[50] This is not to argue that most of the long list of scholars and critics who have considered the film over the course of a century have all misunderstood it; rather it is to suggest simply that such a position is no longer possible, given what we know now. *The Birth of a Nation* has fulfilled a number of functions in the development of film scholarship and film culture, and for a significant portion of that time the true extent of the differences between Griffith's history and the actual history was little known. Nevertheless, over the decades *The Birth of a Nation* has been a useful and necessary object for arguments about the nature of film, the importance of film history, artistic freedom and artistic responsibility. In each epoch, debates about the film have been shaped by the prevailing ideas of the time.

Today, it is no longer possible to set the film's relationship to history aside, which forces us to confront a difficult set of questions about the place of history in fiction films and about the moral responsibility of film-makers. *The Birth of a Nation* is indeed the most extreme example of such a film, so the conclusions we reach from it can be misleading. At the same time, it forces us to acknowledge that historical truth does matter, and that the wide latitude we give to film-makers does indeed have some rigid limits.

2 The Legacy

It is not difficult to imagine audiences in 1915 leaving the theatre deeply inspired by what they had just seen. Griffith had simultaneously created and mastered the type of historical epic that would transport and inspire audiences for at least a century afterwards. It played to the prejudices of most of them, and there would have been few white people who strenuously objected to the content or the message. The acting, *mise en scène*, editing and score had all come together to express an undoubtedly clear vision. Almost all film viewers will have had the experience, at least once in their lives, of walking out of a theatre inspired and awestruck. It is, to some extent, the goal of the endeavour. There is one part of the experience we cannot re-create, however. We can only imagine what it would have been like to see such a film if one had never seen anything remotely like it before. This was, for many who saw it, a new and singular experience. For that reason alone, it would have had an intense and ineffable effect on their hearts and minds. The social and political influence of this film was deep and widespread.

The Birth of a Nation was one of the first films screened at the White House.[51] President Woodrow Wilson had known Thomas Dixon since their university days together, and Dixon asked Wilson to view the film. Since Wilson was still in mourning for his wife (who had died in August 1914), he could not go to the theatre, and so the film was screened at

Advertisement for 1930 re-release that encourages parents to 'Bring the Kiddies'

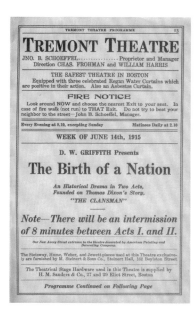

the White House, by some accounts with Griffith and Dixon in attendance. The most famous quotation associated with *The Birth of a Nation* is attributed to this screening – that upon seeing the film, Wilson declared that it was 'Like writing history with lightning', which is followed in some accounts with 'and my only regret is that it is all so terribly true'. There is no evidence that Wilson ever said this. If he had, it would have been discussed at the time or appeared in publicity, but in fact the first written record of these words being directly attributed to him is in a 1937 article in *Scribner's* magazine.[52] There are traces of some debate at the time over whether or not Wilson had endorsed the film. The mere fact that it was shown at the White House could certainly have given that impression.[53] An editorial published in the *Chicago Defender* (an African-American newspaper) on 8 May 1915 reports that Wilson had denied endorsing the film, and that the showing was a favour to an old friend.[54] Since Wilson had himself been cited in the film, it seems unlikely that he would have been overly shocked by its content, whether he actually enjoyed the film or not. He later called it an 'unfortunate production'.[55] His own record on civil rights was not very progressive even for the time – he had re-segregated the federal civil service beginning in 1913.[56]

The film rolled out slowly across the country – Los Angeles and New York first in February and March, Chicago in May and Atlanta in December. It would not play in smaller centres until 1916.

Programme from the Tremont Theatre in Boston, 1915

This was not because of a lack of distribution or demand, but simply because it preserved the special nature of the presentations and helped to keep ticket prices very high. Nearly everywhere it went, controversy followed. The National Association for the Advancement of Colored People led the charge against the film for decades. It is part of the folklore of the film that it caused riots, but there seems to be little evidence of this. There were many protests, and occasional disturbances in theatres and outside, but little actual violence.

Most of the attempts to shut it down happened in courtrooms and in censorship offices, as opponents of the film sought to have it banned.[57] There were numerous censorship boards in 1915, sometimes with overlapping jurisdictions. Their ability to ban films had just been reinforced by the US Supreme Court's *Mutual* decision, which by coincidence was handed down the same month that *The Birth of a Nation* debuted in Los Angeles, having been argued the month before. The case famously held that motion pictures were 'a business, pure and simple' and thus not subject to the provisions of the First Amendment of the US Constitution, which protects freedom of speech and artistic expression.[58] This meant that films could be edited by state and local censorship boards, a situation that remained in effect until the Supreme Court reversed itself in the *Burstyn* decision in 1952.[59]

Each time that *The Birth of a Nation* was banned in a community, Griffith had the resources to deploy lawyers and representatives to make his case, and in almost all instances they succeeded in having the film approved for viewing. Long-time bans were upheld in only a few places, including the state of Ohio. Even there, the film was shown widely, and legally, in 1917 and 1918 before being banned again for decades, only becoming legal in the 1950s after *Burstyn* removed the legal basis for state censorship boards.[60]

Despite the solid legal standing of local censorship boards in 1915, most of the bans failed, because very few boards were able to censor films on the grounds of racism. Censor boards were designed to guard public morals and to protect audiences from images of sexuality, blasphemy or excessive violence, and thus bans demanded by black citizens' groups had to fight an uphill battle. In most cases, the only way to ban a film for racism was to claim that it was in some way a threat to public order. In addition to being difficult to prove, this angle was sometimes itself twisted by racism. To the film's opponents, *The Birth of a Nation* was likely to increase violence against African Americans (and there is indeed some evidence that it did[61]), but in most of the censor board arguments, the expressed fear is that black people will riot over the film, once again portraying African Americans as prone to violence and needing to be controlled. Griffith's lawyers sometimes offered testimonials from chiefs of police in other cities stating that they had had no problems with the black residents of their town, as if that were the real problem with the film.[62] In the abstract, the threat of public disorder is also an example of what later became known as the 'heckler's veto': the ability of someone opposed to a work of art or public speech to have it shut down by claiming that it was inciting them to violence. It is difficult to reconcile such a censorship model with even moderate support for free speech.[63]

As much as we like to discuss the 'impact' of films and other works of art, there are in fact very few examples of a visible effect outside of the world of film itself. There are remarkably few films that manage to stimulate substantial public discussions, influence laws or create other measurable changes. *The Birth of a Nation* drew attention because of its novelty and its content, and as its reputation and notoriety grew, the potential to actively use it to promote racist agendas did not go unnoticed. By the time of the film's release in 1915, the early Ku Klux Klan that had been founded during the Reconstruction was defunct. The rise of Jim Crow laws in the South meant that the Klan's goals had been ensconced in law, and with white supremacy reinforced, there was less and less need for a vigilante organisation to threaten black citizens – the police and justice system would do that themselves. Small steps had been taken

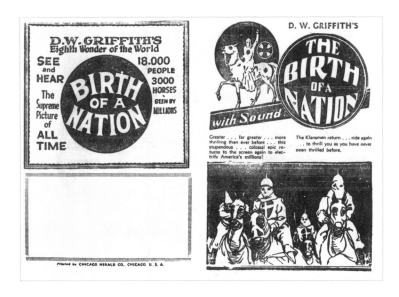

towards racial equality by 1915, including education for black citizens (supposedly 'separate but equal' after the infamous Supreme Court decision in *Plessy* v. *Ferguson* in 1896) and the extension of the voting franchise to black men through the Fifteenth Amendment to the Constitution in 1870. The latter right was difficult to exercise for many, especially in the South, where legal restrictions and outright intimidation kept many African Americans from the polls.

For many Americans, even these small steps to equality were too much. The slow shift towards racial tolerance, coupled with a massive wave of immigration in the late nineteenth and early twentieth centuries, created an overwhelming backlash in the United States. By 1924, a new Ku Klux Klan would be in existence that boasted four million members, making it one of the largest social organisations in the country.[64]

The publicity surrounding *The Birth of a Nation* provided the perfect opportunity for the rebirth of the Klan. On Thanksgiving Day, 25 November 1915, William Joseph Simmons and a small group

Colour flyer for 1930 re-release with images of Klansmen

of followers burned a cross on Stone Mountain, outside Atlanta, to announce the new KKK. *The Birth of a Nation* was to debut in the city a few weeks later, on 6 December, and Simmons was well aware that he could share the film's publicity. He placed an advertisement for his new order in the *Atlanta Journal* alongside the one announcing the film, and later claimed that the order could not have grown the way it did without the help of the film. *The Birth of a Nation* was then used widely throughout the country as a Klan recruiting tool. Sometimes Klan chapters signed members up outside theatres, and sometimes they booked screenings explicitly to enlist new recruits. In a few places, screenings were attended by ushers dressed in Confederate uniforms, or even Klan hoods.[65]

In a 1928 magazine article in which Simmons summarises the ways in which he promoted the Klan on the coat-tails of the film, the author also quotes Griffith responding to Simmons's claim by saying 'That ends a thirteen-year-old mystery':

'I've been accused of having made The Birth of a Nation as propaganda for the Klan. What's more throughout the years I have been constantly asked to explain the relationship between that picture and the Klan. That accusation seemed foolish to me; so did the question. But, if Simmons actually used The Birth of a Nation to raise membership in the Klan, as he says he did, running his Klan advertising simultaneously with advertising of the picture, I can see how many people may have been confused.

'I had no more idea that The Birth of a Nation might be used to revive the old Klan than I might have had that "Intolerance" would revive the ancient persecution of the Huguenots.'[66]

This defence of *The Birth of a Nation* was frequently offered by Griffith, and if to us it seems naive, we must remember that we cannot assume that he or anyone else could have foreseen the film's impact. There was simply no precedent for a single film having the social influence that this one did, and even now it remains a singular example in the history of cinema. Even though Griffith was well

aware of the popularity of cinema, and was consciously trying to
make his audience think and feel as he thought they should, the
power of what he had created seems to have come as a shock
nevertheless. In the same 1928 interview, he claims that 'A terrific
power lies in the motion picture. It's a power that is only too leanly
recognized in these days. I'm constantly amazed and sometimes
almost terrified by it.'[67]

* * *

The sound re-release of *The Birth of a Nation* in 1930 seems to have
been originally envisioned as a talkie of some sort, complete with
dubbed voices. There is a surviving 'script' for this version in the
D. W. Griffith collection of the Museum of Modern Art that
contains dialogue for a number of the crowd scenes, but no synced
dialogue for specific characters. The plan to add dialogue was
abandoned, and the film was released in a much truncated version,
with a musical soundtrack drawn from pieces of its original score

and some sound effects.
More significant were the cuts,
which both rewrote many of
the most inflammatory
intertitles and reduced the film
to an action-adventure epic
with less history and context.
This attempt at giving the film
a second commercial life was
not especially successful.
Movies had changed a lot in
the intervening years, and not
just because of the advent of
sound. The style of films had
also changed significantly –
acting and plots were more
subdued as American drama

A poster for the sound-era re-release of the film, 1930

continued its slow shift from the primacy of melodrama to a realism that appeared more naturalistic.

Even if its commercial rebirth was not to be, *The Birth of a Nation* was about to begin a second life that would have been difficult to imagine before 1915. Beginning in the late 1920s, there were occasional retrospectives of earlier films, as the medium was now ready to move beyond a focus on the newest to allow for some consideration of what had been made in the past – the beginnings of film history as an idea. The biggest step in the US came in 1935 with the founding of the film library at the Museum of Modern Art in New York. At first, the library did not have a permanent home – it held screenings around New York and offered a collection of circulating prints. *The Birth of Nation* and *Intolerance* were staples of this circuit from the earliest days, and soon after its permanent home opened in 1940, MoMA offered the earliest retrospective of Griffith's work. His contributions to the development of narrative cinema made him an easy choice for a retrospective, but the museum also had to deal with the racism of his most famous work, which seemed extreme by 1940, at least in New York cultural circles. To complicate matters further, the museum's film library was under intense pressure in 1940 to demonstrate that it was sufficiently American. It had faced repeated and pointed questions about the 'foreignness' of both its staff and the films it showed, and one of its employees, Jay Leyda, had been labelled a 'soviet propagandist' because he had spent time in the USSR studying film-making with Sergei Eisenstein and Dziga Vertov. Griffith himself wrote to Nelson Rockefeller and asked that film library director Iris Barry be replaced for the purposes of this exhibit by Griffith's own brother.[68] In that context, the title of the exhibit, 'American Film Master', and the downplaying of the film's racism in catalogue materials seem in part calculated to present the museum as sufficiently friendly to Hollywood and mainstream America.

In the 1950s and 60s, hundreds of amateur cinema clubs sprang up in the United States and around the world. These were clubs for cinephiles who organised screenings of historical or artistic films. Since *The Birth of a Nation* was a key film in cinema history, many of these groups showed the film at some point, rarely without controversy. In surviving programmes and letters culled from archives, we can trace their arguments about how they see cinema and what it means to them. Just at the moment where changing attitudes about race make *The Birth of a Nation* less socially acceptable, film is becoming recognised as an art form. This means that although the film is no longer defensible as American history, it is now defensible as *film history*, a category of history that did not previously exist. This is a key shift, because it changes the terms of the debate. No longer are we defending Griffith because he told an unfortunate truth, but because the film itself is historically important.[69]

This perspective was later adopted by film academics as university film programmes grew in the 1960s. Even while many programmes were oriented towards production, there was a strong sense that film now had canonical works that should be studied. In the case of *The Birth of a Nation*, this created a dilemma, since the film was so important in terms of the development of film form. The 'solution' in many classrooms was to ask students simply to ignore the racist content and pay attention to the cinematography and editing. In practice, however, form and content are not so easily separable. Teachers' advice to set aside the racism was a choice to ignore what is so fascinating and troubling about the film. We can perhaps attribute this choice in part to cinema's tenuous place in the university system, an inherently conservative culture where cinema was attempting to find a place alongside English and art history. To belong, film needed masterpieces, and preferably old ones. *The Birth of a Nation* fitted the bill, even if that meant being less than honest about the film's message. Obviously, there was no one way of teaching *The Birth of a Nation*, and some teachers submitted it to withering critique. But available evidence suggests that glossing over its racist content was far more common, at least in the earliest days.[70] Beginning around the late 1980s and early 90s, academic film

criticism became more and more concerned with representations of race on film, and the tenor of discussion of the film changed considerably as scholars became highly attuned to the subtleties and complexities of these representations. The more stable position of cinema studies as an academic discipline meant that foundational works could be subjected to more substantial critique.

In the twenty-first century, *The Birth of a Nation* was relevant again, this time at the intersection of art and remix culture. The film was the subject of a live remix performance by DJ Spooky (real name: Paul Miller) that toured museums and performance spaces around the world beginning in 2004. The film's frames were combined with music, contemporary media images and voiceover to critique its racism and to underscore the continuities between the film's views and contemporary politics. Miller called his remix project (which was performed live each night and thus varied slightly with each performance) a 'digital exorcism', where he was trying to confront the images and 'make them absurd'.[71] The combination of a film and music remix was innovative in 2004, and involved, as

DJ Spooky performs *Rebirth of a Nation*, 20 November 2004 (Photo by Michal Raz-Russo, © Museum of Contemporary Art Chicago)

Miller said, 'thinking about how people move between media like moving between different languages', a movement that represented a process of 'creolization'.[72] Such combinations became much more common in the decade after Miller's project, especially after the launch of YouTube in 2005, which allowed amateur versions of remixes to be easily shared. Ten years after DJ Spooky started performing what came to be called *Rebirth of a Nation*, there were numerous *Birth of a Nation* remixes online, many apparently made by student film-makers.

An educational CD-ROM published by W. W. Norton in 2004 also encouraged students to remix scenes of the film as a way of understanding the power of the imagery, and to consider how the order of shots or the content of the intertitles could change the message of the film.[73] Obviously, much of the racist content of the film is in the titles, and if these were rewritten to encourage viewers to read the images of plantation life critically instead of sympathetically, it would be a very different film. As we have noted, the racism is also inscribed in the bodies of the white actors who perform in blackface, and trying to re-purpose these scenes is more complicated. Video remix can be a powerful tool of critique, and a full consideration of its possibilities is only just getting under way.[74] In the early twenty-first century, video remix seems to be regarded much as music remixing and sampling was in the 1980s, as interesting and fun but not something to be taken seriously in its own right. DJ Spooky is obviously not in this category, having been invited to present his version of the film all over the world. But most remixers work alone with considerably less praise and feedback, even though video-sharing sites provide a showcase for their work, and audiences can be quite large. The medium has significant political potential, as some of the control over images of women and minorities passes out of the hands of those who can afford to make films and into the hands of those who are the subjects of these images.

In the century since *The Birth of a Nation* appeared, multiple generations of black film-makers have taken up cameras, trying to correct, in part, the damage done by this film and others. The most famous of these is Oscar Micheaux, who made numerous films beginning in the late 1910s and 20s that do not simply include positive images of African Americans, but in many cases present a much more sophisticated and nuanced view of the possibilities of filmic truth.[75] Micheaux and the black film-makers who followed him had to deal with the challenges of funding films and of finding an audience despite being shut out of the studio system and mainstream distribution. In the early 1980s, when he was a film student at New York University, Spike Lee remembers being shown *The Birth of a Nation* as a stylistic example for students to learn from. In Lee's first student film, *The Answer* (1980), a black film-maker is offered $50 million to shoot a remake of *The Birth of a Nation*. It apparently offended some professors, who saw it as an attack on a master, and Lee was nearly kicked out of the programme. Lee's career since that time has included making films that challenge stereotypes of African Americans and sometimes focus on important chapters in black history. He also ended up back at NYU as the artistic director of the graduate film programme[76] that had nearly ejected him.

* * *

In late 2012, some of the cast and crew of Steven Spielberg's film *Lincoln* were invited by President Obama to a special screening of their work at the White House. The event provided a compelling counterpoint to the screening of *The Birth of a Nation* there nearly a century before. Here was another film about Abraham Lincoln being shown at the White House, and to the first African-American president. The contrast was a poignant one, given that the United States still has a long way to go on its path to the racial harmony it has long sought. Nevertheless, it was difficult not to see it as a milestone that would have been unimaginable in 1915, when cinema was so new, and the spirit of Lincoln's promises of freedom seemed far away indeed.

Notes

1 D. W. Griffith, 'Reply to the *New York Globe*', 10 April 1915. Reprinted in Robert Lang (ed.), *The Birth of a Nation: D. W. Griffith, Director* (New Brunswick, NJ: Rutgers University Press, 1994), p. 168.

2 Given that there were no centralised box-office figures in 1915–16, it is impossible to know, and estimates vary widely. Tickets were often $1–$2 (the equivalent of $24–$48 in 2015). On the other hand, the population of the USA in 1915 was only about 100 million.

3 To point to just one famous example, many people have noticed that the *mise en scène* of some of the rally scenes in *The Triumph of the Will* neatly matches that of the final sequence of *Star Wars: A New Hope* (1977), in which Luke Skywalker and his friends receive their medals. The point is not that *Star Wars* has fascist undertones, but that crowds can gather to celebrate any type of cause.

4 The film was often marketed with numbers that emphasised its scope: '8,000 extras!' Many of these numbers have been cited in relation to the film ever since, but are impossible to confirm, and there is no scene in *The Birth of a Nation* that seems to use more than a few hundred extras. Even if no one appeared more than once, which is unlikely, there are nowhere near 8,000 extras in the film. Most accounts of the filming refer to actors playing multiple roles.

5 Clyde Taylor has pointed out that 'For obscure reasons, narrative works considered landmarks in American culture for technical innovation and/or popular success have often importantly involved the portrayal of African Americans.' He cites *The Jazz Singer* (1927), *Gone with the Wind* (1939), *Song of the South* (1946) and *Roots* (1977), in addition to *The Birth of a Nation*. Taylor, 'The Re-Birth of the Aesthetic in Cinema', in David Bernardi (ed.), *The Birth of Whiteness: Race and the Emergence of U.S. Cinema* (New Brunswick, NJ: Rutgers University Press, 1996), p. 15.

6 See, for example, Francis Hackett, 'Brotherly Love', *New Republic* vol. 7 (20 March 1915), p. 185, and 'Capitalizing Race Hatred', *New York Globe*, 6 April 1915. Both reprinted in Lang, *Birth of a Nation*, pp. 161–5.

7 See, for example, Henry Stephen Gordon, 'The Story of David Wark Griffith (Part V)', *Photoplay* vol. x no. 5 (October 1916), p. 94; Gordon, 'The Real Story of "Intolerance"', *Photoplay* vol. x no. 6 (November 1916), p. 34; Lillian Gish (with Ann Pinchot), *The Movies, Mr. Griffith, and Me* (Englewood Cliffs, NJ: Prentice-Hall, 1969), pp. 163–5.

8 There is a good bibliography on *The Birth of a Nation* by Daniel Bernardi and Michelle J. Martinez that is part of the online *Oxford Bibliographies*. A free bibliography is available from the University of California, Berkeley, at: <http://www.lib.berkeley.edu/MRC/GriffithBib.html#birth>. For an overview of major debates and sources, see the essays on *The Birth of a Nation* in Paolo Cherchi Usai (ed.), *The Griffith Project, Vol. 8: Films Produced in 1914–15* (London: BFI, 2004).

9 'The Birth of a Nation', *New York Times*, 4 March 1915.

10 Griffith, 'Reply to the *New York Globe*, p. 169.

11 In his biography of Griffith, Richard Schickel suggests that much of the work on this version was done by Harry and Roy Aitken, two of Griffith's long-time producers and partners. Schickel, *D. W. Griffith: An American Life* (New York: Simon & Schuster, 1984), p. 555.

12 Richard Barry, 'Five-Dollar Movies Prophesied', *Editor* vol. 40 (24 April 1915), p. 409. Cited in Introduction to Fred Silva (ed.), *Focus on The Birth of a Nation* (Englewood Cliffs, NJ: Prentice-Hall, 1971), p. 10.

13 The truth status of written history has been the subject of ferocious debate in recent years. Key texts include Peter Novick, *That Noble Dream: The 'Objectivity Question' and the American Historical Profession* (Cambridge: Cambridge University Press, 1988), and Hayden White, *The Content of the Form: Narrative Discourse and Historical Representation* (Baltimore, MD: Johns Hopkins University Press, 1987). For a counterpoint, see Keith Windschuttle, *The Killing of History* (San Francisco: Encounter, 1996). See also Paul McEwan, *Knowledge and the Limits of Postmodernism: Social Constructionism in Film and Media Studies*, doctoral dissertation, Northwestern University (Ann Arbor: ProQuest/UMI, 2003).

14 See John David Smith and J. Vincent Lowery (eds), *The Dunning School: Historians, Race, and the Meaning of Reconstruction* (Lexington: University Press of Kentucky, 2013).

15 Charles S. Druggan and Charles J. Trainor, *In Support of Application of Epoch Producing Corporation in Re: 'Birth of a Nation'* (1925). Collection of the Ohio State Archives, Columbus, Ohio. For more details, see Paul McEwan, 'Lawyers, Bibliographies, and the Klan: Griffith's Resources in the Censorship Battle over *The Birth of a Nation* in Ohio', *Film History* vol. 20 (2008), pp. 357–66. A complete list of the sources in the bibliography is: Woodrow Wilson (*History of the American People: Division and Reunion*); Walter L. Fleming, Professor of History, West Virginia University (*Documentary History of Reconstruction*); Samuel L. McCall (*Life of Thaddeus Stevens*); John W. Burgess, Professor of Political Science and Constitutional Law, Columbia University (*Reconstruction and the Constitution*); Julian Hawthorne, 'son of Nathaniel' (*Hawthorne's United States*); James W. Garner, Fellow at Columbia University (*Reconstruction in Mississippi*); Hillery A. Herbert (*Why the Solid South*); Professor Hart, Harvard University (*Reconstruction of the South*). No publication details are offered for these works in the bibliography.

16 The film lists only 'Nicolay and Hay', since their ten-volume biography of Lincoln, published twenty-five years before, was already well known. The two men were Lincoln's secretaries.

17 Tom Gunning, *D. W. Griffith and the Origins of American Narrative Film: The Early Years at Biograph* (Urbana: University of Illinois Press, 1991), pp. 42–3.

18 For an overview of the difficulties in determining which surviving copy is closest to what would have been seen in 1915, see the introduction to John Cuniberti's *'The Birth of a Nation'*:

A Formal Shot-by-Shot Analysis Together with Microfiche (Woodbridge, CT: Research Publications, 1979), and J. B. Kaufman, 'Non-Archival Sources', in Cherchi Usai, *Griffith Project, Vol. 8*, pp. 107–12.

19 For a discussion of the same issues in relation to Griffith's *Intolerance*, see Russell Merritt, 'D. W. Griffith's *Intolerance*: Reconstructing an Unattainable Text', *Film History* vol. 4 (1990), pp. 337–75.

20 Vivian Sobchack, '"Surge and Splendor": A Phenomenology of the Hollywood Historical Epic', *Representations* no. 29 (Winter 1990), p. 26.

21 Ibid.

22 It is included in the most recent three-disc Kino Video version (2011).

23 Griffith, 'Reply to the *New York Globe*', p. 169.

24 The case was *Loving* v. *Virginia (Richard Perry Loving, Mildred Jeter Loving* v. *Virginia)*. 388 U.S. 1. Argued 10 April 1967. Decided 12 June 1967. It struck down Virginia's Racial Integrity Act, which had been passed in 1924, and simultaneously invalidated fifteen other state bans on interracial marriage.

25 See John Meacham, *Thomas Jefferson: The Art of Power* (New York: Random House, 2012).

26 Benjamin Quarles, *The Negro in the Civil War* (New York: Da Capo Press, 1989 [1953]), p. 119.

27 See Ira Berlin, Joseph P. Reidy and Leslie S. Rowland (eds), *Freedom's Soldiers: The Black Military Experience in the Civil War* (Cambridge: Cambridge University Press, 1998).

28 See Schickel, *D. W. Griffith*, p. 555.

29 [The Birth of a Nation – Outtakes and Production Footage] Library of Congress (AFI/Killiam Collection) [LC item numbers FPA 0048-0049]. For more details, see Mike Mashon, '[Production Footage of The Birth of a Nation]', *Griffith Project, Vol. 8*, p. 49.

30 Thomas Dixon Jr, *The Clansman: An Historical Romance of the Ku Klux Klan* (New York: Grosset and Dunlap, 1905), p. 8.

31 In his biography of Griffith, Martin Williams quotes Griffith as having 'once said' of blacks: 'They were our children, whom we loved and cared for all our lives.' There is no citation for this reference in Williams's book, but it fits the tone of Griffith's perspectives on race. Williams, *Griffith: First Artist of the Movies* (New York: Oxford University Press, 1980), p. 78.

32 For examples, see note 15 on Druggan and Trainor bibliography.

33 Booker T. Washington. 'Up from Slavery' (1901). Collected in Anthony Appiah (ed.), *Early African-American Classics* (New York: Bantam Books, 1990), pp. 330–1.

34 Ibid., p. 327.

35 Gish (with Ann Pinchot), *The Movies, Mr. Griffith and Me*, p. 99.

36 Mimi White, '*The Birth of a Nation*: History as Pretext', in Lang, *Birth of a Nation*, p. 218.

37 For more detailed discussion of the ways in which race, class and slave ownership intersected in cases of rape, see Diane Miller Sommerville, *Rape and Race in the Nineteenth-Century South* (Chapel Hill: University of North Carolina Press, 2004).

38 Wilson's book encloses the phrase 'put the white South under the heel of the black South' in quotation marks, but it is not attributed to anyone in particular, only to 'men who had followed [Thaddeus] Stevens'. Stevens is the politician upon whom Austin Stoneman is based. Wilson, *A History of the American People, Vol. 5* (New York: Harper and Brothers, 1903), pp. 49–50.

39 In a discussion of the film *Braveheart* (1995), Colin McArthur explores some of the uses of Scottish nationalism among white supremacists in the American South. McArthur, 'It Takes One to Know One: *Braveheart*'s Appeal to the Proto-Fascist Psyche', in *Braveheart, Brigadoon, and the Scots: Distortions of Scotland in Hollywood Cinema* (London: I. B. Tauris, 2003), pp. 192–208.

40 W. Stephen Bush, 'The Birth of a Nation', *Motion Picture World*, 13 March 1915, pp. 1586–7.

41 See Anthony Slide, *Hollywood Unknowns: A History of Extras, Bit Players, and Stand-Ins* (Jackson: University Press of Mississippi, 2012), pp. 195–6.

42 This character is not named in the film, and in various sources he has two different names and several actor credits. The character who recites these lines is called Jake in the novel of *The Clansman* and Nelse in the stage version. Some sources, including versions of the programme dating from 1915 and 1916, mistakenly list these as two different characters. The role of 'Nelse, an old-fashioned negro' is attributed to William DeVaull, and the role of 'Jake, a black man faithful unto death' to William Freeman. In fact, Freeman played the sentry at the hospital who moons after Lillian Gish (see Karl Brown, *Adventures with D. W. Griffith* [New York: Farrar, Straus and Giroux, 1973], p. 92). Several sources from 1915 and 1916 mention DeVaull's role in *The Birth of a Nation*, although not by character name. For example, *Motography* of 6 May 1916 notes that 'William de Vaull [sic], who was one of the prominent negro slaves in "The Birth of a Nation" plays a colored servant in a Kentucky story Allan Dwan is directing with Lillian Gish as star. Sam de Grasse, Jennie Lee, and Spottiswodde [sic] Aitken are in the cast' (p. 1061). All of these actors were in *The Birth of a Nation*. That film became *An Innocent Magdalene* (1916), which was written by Griffith and is now considered lost. To complicate matters further, a biography of British-born vaudeville performer Harry Braham attributes the role to him (Janet Muir, *Masks and Faces: The Life and Career of Harry Braham* [Gosport, Hants.: Chaplin Books, 2014]). Braham apparently told his family that he had played the role in the film, and surviving photographs reveal a strong resemblance, but there is no outside evidence for his participation, other than his obituary in *Variety* on 27 September 1923 (p. 9), which says that 'In later years he worked steadily for D.W. Griffith in pictures until illness overtook him', but offers no more specifics. The best evidence though is the scene is which Jake, the 'faithful family servant' is 'punished for not voting with the Union League and Carpetbaggers'. One of the white actors in blackface (wearing striped overalls) who entices Jake out of the house and hands him over to the troops appears to be William DeVaull, while Jake appears to be Harry Braham.

43 Gordon, 'David Wark Griffith (Part V)', p. 94.

44 For an overview, see Stephen Johnson (ed.), *Burnt Cork: Traditions and Legacies of Blackface Minstrelsy* (Amherst: University of Massachusetts Press, 2012).

45 The most recent and complete edition of the film (Kino Video, 2011) has a new score not based on the original. While it is a much more complete print, it loses much by not having at least a version of the Breil score.

46 See Daniel Barenboim, 'Those Who Want to Leave, Do So', *Guardian*, Friday 6 September 2002. Available at: <http://www.theguardian.com/music/2002/sep/06/classicalmusicandopera.artsfeatures>. Accessed 3 December 2013. Terry Teachout, 'Why Israel Still Shuts Wagner Out', *Wall Street Journal*, 31 January 2009. Available at: <http://online.wsj.com/news/articles/SB123335355844034825>. Accessed 3 December 2013. Harriet Sherwood, 'Tel Aviv Wagner Concert Cancelled after Wave of Protest', *Guardian*, 5 June 2012. Available at: <http://www.theguardian.com/world/2012/jun/05/tel-aviv-wagner-concert-cancelled>. Accessed 3 December 2013.

47 Allyson Field, 'Before and After *The Birth of a Nation*: Motion Picture Production at Hampton Institute (1913–1915)', in *Filming Uplift and Projecting Possibility* (Durham, NC: Duke University Press, 2015).

48 See White, *Content of the Form*.

49 See also Robert C. Allen and Douglas Gomery, *Film History: Theory and Practice* (New York: Knopf, 1985).

50 Arthur Lennig's 2004 article in the journal *Film History* is an unfortunate example here. Lennig is a trustworthy historian when it comes to film history, correcting a number of persistent myths about the film. When it comes to American history, though, he ignores the decline of the Dunning school and virtually all scholarship on the Reconstruction written in the past fifty years, quoting without comment Woodrow Wilson's justifications for the Klan in his *History of the American People*, and accepting at face value Griffith's defence that he had presented 'three Negroes faithful unto death' and thus his film was not racist. Lennig, 'Myth and Fact: The Reception of *The Birth of a Nation*', *Film History* vol. 16 (2004), pp. 126, 139.

51 Although *The Birth of a Nation* is frequently referred to as the first film shown at the White House, that honour seems to have gone to *Cabiria* (1914), which was shown on the White House lawn while Woodrow Wilson and his family watched from a porch in 1914. Mark Benbow, 'Wilson the Man', in Ross A. Kennedy (ed.), *A Companion to Woodrow Wilson* (Malden, MA: John Wiley & Sons, 2013), p. 29.

52 Milton MacKaye, '*The Birth of a Nation*', *Scribner's* vol. 102 no. 5 (November 1937), p. 69. See also Lennig, 'Myth and Fact', p. 122.

53 Biographer John Milton Cooper says that Wilson 'fell into the trap' laid by

Dixon, who knew the President's endorsement would be valuable. Cooper, *Woodrow Wilson: A Biography* (New York: Random House, 2009), pp. 272–3.

54 Unsigned and untitled editorial, *Chicago Defender*, 8 May 1915, p. 8. The full text reads: 'President Wilson emphatically denies that he has put his O.K. on *The Birth of a Nation*. Its exhibition at the White House was a courtesy extended the author, who was a classmate of his at Johns Hopkins University, he avers. We take great pleasure in erasing one demerit mark from our high chief and suggest that if it isn't too painful, he might keep the good work up.'

55 A. Scott Berg, *Wilson* (New York: Putnam, 2013), p. 349.

56 Deanna Boyd and Kendra Chen, 'The History and Experience of African Americans in America's Postal Service', Smithsonian National Postal Museum, Washington, DC. Available at: <http://postalmuseum.si.edu/AfricanAmericanHistory/p5.html>. Accessed 8 January 2014.

57 There are several book-length overviews of the film's censorship history. The most recent is Dick Lehr's *The Birth of a Nation: How a Legendary Filmmaker and a Crusading Editor Reignited America's Civil War* (New York: Public Affairs, 2014), which focuses primarily on the years immediately after the film's release. Melvyn Stokes's excellent *D. W. Griffith's The Birth of a Nation: A History of 'The Most Controversial Motion Picture of All Time'* (New York: Oxford University Press, 2007) follows the film

over several decades. There is also the published dissertation by Nickieann Fleener-Marzec, *D. W. Griffith's The Birth of a Nation: Controversy, Suppression, and the First Amendment as It Applies to Filmic Expression, 1915–1973* (New York: Arno Press, 1980).

58 *Mutual Film Corporation* v. *Industrial Commission of Ohio*. Appeal from the District Court of the United States for the Northern District of Ohio. No. 456. Argued 6–7 January 1915. Decided 23 February 1915, p. 1.

59 *Joseph Burstyn, Incorporated* v. *Wilson, Commissioner of Education of New York, et al.* 343 U.S. 495. Argued 24 April 1952. Decided 26 May 1952.

60 See McEwan, 'Lawyers, Bibliographies, and the Klan', pp. 357–66.

61 See Maxim Simcovitch, 'The Impact of Griffith's *Birth of a Nation* on the Modern Ku Klux Klan', *Journal of Popular Film and Television* vol. 1 no.1 (1972), pp. 45–54. Reprinted in David Platt (ed.), *Celluloid Power: Social Film Criticism from The Birth of a Nation to Judgement at Nuremberg* (Metuchen, NJ: Scarecrow Press, 1992), pp. 72–82.

62 These documents are preserved in the Ohio State Archives, Columbus, Ohio.

63 The most famous case related to the 'heckler's veto' is *Irving Feiner* v. *New York*. 340 U.S. 315. Argued 17 October 1950. Decided 15 January 1951. Feiner was arrested for a political speech on a Syracuse street in 1949 because the police claimed that the crowd listening was getting out of control. His conviction was upheld by the Supreme Court. Feiner was speaking on the street because Syracuse mayor

Frank Costello had refused a permit for a meeting at a public school auditorium. Only a couple of months later, Costello would also deny permission for *The Birth of a Nation* to be shown in Syracuse.

64 Wyn Craig Wade, *The Fiery Cross: The Ku Klux Klan in America* (New York: Oxford University Press, 1987), p. 253.

65 See Simcovitch, 'Impact of Griffith's *Birth of a Nation*', pp. 45–54. For histories of the early days of Simmons's Klan, see Scott Cutlip, *The Unseen Power: Public Relations, a History* (Hillsdale, NJ: Lawrence Erlbaum Associates, 1994), pp. 372–8, and Wade, *The Fiery Cross*, pp. 119–39.

66 William G. Shepherd, 'How I Put over The Klan', *Collier's Magazine*, 14 July 1928, p. 35.

67 Ibid.

68 Haidee Wasson, *Museum Movies: The Museum of Modern Art and the Birth of Art Cinema* (Berkeley: University of California Press, 2005), pp. 181–2.

69 The John Griggs Collection (papers on *The Birth of a Nation*), collection of Trexler Library, Muhlenberg College, Allentown, Pennsylvania. There are also significant documents in the collection of the Cinémathèque Québécoise in Montreal.

70 A lot of this evidence is, by its nature, anecdotal. I have had dozens of conversations over the years with people who were professors and students during this period, and many share, unprompted, their recollections of being taught about the film when I describe my research interests. The discipline-wide tendency to gloss over the racism is also evidenced in the writing of the period – there was very little critique of the film's politics.

71 Author interview with Paul Miller, 13 June 2004.

72 Ibid.

73 Ellen Strain and Gregory VanHoosier-Carey, with Patrick Ledwell and Patrick Quattlebaum, *Griffith in Context: A Multimedia Exploration of* The Birth of a Nation (CD-ROM) (New York: Films in Context/W. W. Norton, 2004).

74 See, for example, the journal *Transformative Works and Cultures*. Available at: <http://journal.transformativeworks.org/index.php/twc>.

75 This observation comes from a presentation by Ariel Rogers. See also Pearl Bowser, Jane Gaines and Charles Musser (eds), *Oscar Micheaux and His Circle* (Bloomington: Indiana University Press, 2001).

76 John Colapinto, 'Barack Changes Everything' (interview with Spike Lee), *Observer*, 4 January 2009. Available at: <http://www.theguardian.com/film/2009/jan/04/spike-lee-interview-john-colapinto>. Accessed 22 January 2014.

Credits

The Birth of a Nation/ The Clansman
USA/1915

Produced under the Personal Direction of
D. W. Griffith
Produced Exclusively by
D. W. Griffith
Adapted from the novels *The Clansman* and *The Leopard's Spots*, and the play *The Clansman* by Thomas Dixon
Story Arranged by
D. W. Griffith
Photography
G. W. (Billy) Bitzer

©1915. David W. Griffith Corporation
©1915. Epoch Producing Corporation and Thomas Dixon
Production Company
Griffith Feature Films

Costumes
Goldstein Co. (Los Angeles)

uncredited
Production Company
Majestic Motion Picture Company
Executive Producers
D. W. Griffith
Harry E. Aitken

Executive/Producing Assistant to D. W. Griffith
J. A. Barry
Scenarists
D. W. Griffith and Frank E. Woods
Based on the novels *The Clansman: An Historical Romance of the Ku Klux Klan* and *The Leopard's Spots*, and the play *The Clansman* by Thomas F. Dixon Jr
Assistant Directors
Thomas E. O'Brien
George André Beranger
George Siegmann
Raoul Walsh
W. S. Van Dyke
Erich von Stroheim
Jack Conway
Monte Blue
William Christy Cabanne
Elmer Clifton
Donald Crisp
Howard Gaye
Fred Hamer
Herbert Sutch
Tom Wilson
Baron von Winther
Allan Dwan
Henry B. Walthall
Camera Operator
Karl Brown
Camera Assistant
Frank B. Good
Special Effects Supervisor
Walter Hoffman

Editor
D. W. Griffith
Assistant Film Editors
Joseph Henabery
Raoul Walsh
Negative Cutters
James Smith
Rose Smith
Set Designer
Frank Wortman
Property Master
Ralph M. DeLacy
Assistant Properties
Hal Sullivan
Construction Co-ordinator
Joseph Stringer
Lead Carpenter
Shorty English
Carpenter
Jim Newman
Set Painter
Cash Shockey
Costumes
Robert Goldstein
Clare West
Musical Accompaniment Composed by
Joseph Carl Breil
D. W. Griffith
Stunt Co-ordinator
Fred Hamer
Unit Publicist
Henry I. McMahon

CAST
Lillian Gish
Elsie Stoneman
Mae Marsh
Flora Cameron, the
pet sister
Henry [B.] Walthall
Colonel Benjamin
Cameron, 'The Little
Colonel'
Miriam Cooper
Margaret Cameron,
elder sister
Mary Alden
Lydia Brown, Stoneman's
housekeeper
Ralph Lewis
The Hon. Austin
Stoneman, Leader of
the House
George Siegmann
Silas Lynch
Walter Long
Gus, the renegade
Wallace Reid
Jeff, the blacksmith
Jos. [Joseph] Henabery
President Abraham
Lincoln
Elmer Clifton
Phil Stoneman, elder son
Josephine Crowell
Mrs Cameron
Spottiswoode Aitken
Dr Cameron
**J. A. Beringer [George
André Beranger]**
Wade Cameron, second
son

Maxfield Stanley
Duke Cameron, youngest
son
Jennie Lee
Mammy, the faithful
servant
Donald Crisp
General Ulysses S. Grant
Howard Gaye
General Robert E. Lee

uncredited
Violet Wilkey
Flora Cameron as a child
Robert Harron
Tod Stoneman, younger
son/spy in
blackface/others
Sam De Grasse
Senator Charles Sumner
Alberta Lee
Mrs Mary Todd Lincoln
William Freeman
mooning sentry at
Federal hospital
Olga Grey
Laura Keene
Raoul Walsh
John Wilkes Booth
Elmo Lincoln
'White-arm' Joe, ginmill
owner/slave auctioneer
(prologue)/others
Tom Wilson
Stoneman's servant
Eugene Pallette
Union soldier
Madame Sul-Te-Wan
woman with gypsy shawl

Harry Braham
Jake/Nelse [see note 42]
Lenore Cooper
Elsie's maid
Alma Rubens
Donna Montran
belles of 1861
Charles Stevens
volunteer who reports
raid on Piedmont
Fred Burns
Allan Sears
Klansmen
Gibson Gowland
Alberta Franklin
Charles King
Monte Blue
William E. Cassidy

Filmed from 4 July to
24 September 1914 on
location in Calexico,
Big Bear Lake, Burbank,
Del Monte, Fullerton,
Los Angeles, Ojai and
Whittier (California,
USA). 35mm; 1.33:1;
black & white; silent.

US theatrical release by
Epoch Producing
Corporation in Los
Angeles (as *The
Clansman*) on 8 February
1915. Running time:
190 minutes; length
c. 13,058 feet/3,980
metres – projected at
16fps (thirteen reels)
US theatrical release by
Epoch Producing

Corporation in New York City (as *The Birth of a Nation*) on 3 March 1915. Subsequently censored, with a running time of c. 165 minutes; length c. 11,581 feet/3,530 metres – projected at 16fps (twelve reels) US theatrical re-release in New York in May 1921 US theatrical re-release in New York on 18 December 1930. Running time: c. 135 minutes (nine reels) US theatrical re-release by Joseph Brenner Associates in 1970 UK theatrical release by Western Import Co. Ltd in 1915. Length 12,000 feet/3,658 metres

Copyrighted under the title **The Birth of the Nation: Or The Clansman** Re-released in an unauthorised abbreviated version as **In the Clutches of the Ku Klux Klan**

Note Original prints display no credits beyond those of Griffith, Dixon and the production companies. Subsequent releases of the film were accompanied by brochures produced by Epoch Producing Corp. which contained cast and credit information.

Credits compiled by Julian Grainger

B F I

BFI Film and TV Classics

Have you read them all?

Each book in the BFI Film and TV Classics series honours a landmark of world cinema and television. With new titles publishing every year, the series offers some of the best writing on film and television available today.

Find out more about this series at **www.palgrave.com/bfi**

palgrave